Out of the
Shadows

Out of the Shadows

MYTHS AND TRUTHS OF MODERN WICCA

Lilith McLelland

CITADEL PRESS
Kensington Publishing Corp.
www.kensingtonbooks.com

CITADEL PRESS BOOKS are published by

Kensington Publishing Corp.
850 Third Avenue
New York, NY 10022

All Kensington titles, imprints, and distributed lines are available at special quantity discounts for bulk purchases for sales promotions, premiums, fund-raising, educational, or institutional use. Special book excerpts or customized printings can also be created to fit specific needs. For details, write or phone the office of the Kensington special sales manager: Kensington Publishing Corp., 850 Third Avenue, New York, NY 10022, attn: Special Sales Department, phone 1-800-221-2647.

Citadel Press and the Citadel Logo are trademarks of Kensington Publishing Corp.

First printing: September 2002

10 9 8 7 6 5 4 3 2 1

Printed in the United States of America

Library of Congress Control Number: 2002100680

ISBN 0-8065-2210-0

Kerowyn and Tiernan of the Clan of the Dragon
Jane, of the Temple of Brigantia
Cassius Julianus of Nova Roma and the Julian Society
Morgan, Selket, Brighid, Renda, and Thorn of the McFarland Dianics
Bryan, Stasi, and Traci of the Order of the Inner Circle
Maeven of Betwixt and Between
Seshet, of the Iseum of Hidden Mysteries
Carol, who was lost but now is found

———

Thanks to all of you for your help and support,
and for your efforts on behalf of our religion.

You guys rule!

Contents

Out of the Shadows

1

What Your Mama Didn't Tell You About Wicca

If you're just coming into Wicca, I really envy you.

Right about now, you're basking in the glow of a new circle of friends unlike any you've known before, you're learning magic (or, as you've probably been cautioned to spell it, *magick,* so nobody will think you're Penn and/or Teller), you've bought a bunch of neat stuff including a black cape, and you sign your e-mails with "Blessed Be."

Those were the days, you betcha.

And now you've run into a bitchy old curmudgeon like me, who's about to tell you that it ain't all bright blessings and white light.

Sometimes, it's just toil and trouble all damn day long.

Witch Wars, job discrimination, unprincipled "high priestesses" running teaching or initiation rackets, people treating your religion as a joke, religious historians bashing Gerald Gardner, anthropologists bashing Margaret Murray, your family on your butt because you don't want to have your kid baptized, and people who insist that you can't be a *real* Witch unless you've been initiated into a coven or born into a "Witch family."

3

And in the middle of all this, some fresh-faced zealot knocks on your door to give you his "testimony" and deliver the happy news that you're going to hell, ya heathen.

But wait! There's an upside to all this.

When you strip away the silliness that has attached itself to Wicca in the last few years, you're uncovering a new, vital religion that's in the painful but rewarding process of reinventing itself. Wiccans are digging out the real truths and discarding the conventional wisdom of Wicca, the misinformation that we ourselves have unwittingly—well, mostly unwittingly—perpetrated. Wicca is growing fast and becoming more visible. Its believers are making inroads into the mainstream of religious thought, while keeping the unique and appealing characteristic of honoring individuality.

Since Wicca became a legal religion in the United States in 1986, Wiccans have been pushing for the "mainstream-ization" of the religion, the recognition of Wicca as a spiritual path as valid as Christianity, Judaism, or Buddhism. Wiccans have done countless media interviews, been guests on talk shows, written impassioned letters to producers of TV shows who have portrayed Wicca either truthfully or erroneously, passed out literature on street corners, talked to law enforcement officials to let them know that the religion is not a cult, and even filed lawsuits on the basis of civil-rights infringement. Wiccan Web sites proliferate like fleas on a Mississippi hound dog.

Wicca has accomplished part of its goal: It has gotten noticed. And there's good news . . . and bad news. The good news is that more and more people are getting the right idea about us. The bad news is that many people have joined what they call "the Craft" (as opposed to "the religion") because, to them, it represents a slap in the face of society, a way to get noticed, or a substitute for therapy. Until we make it clear to our coveners, students, and potential seekers that we are about *religion,* not just magic, and until we stop allowing ourselves be used by the media as "occult" or "spooky," until we stop traipsing around graveyards for the benefit of the cameras, Wicca is in danger of losing its dignity and much of its spiritual effectiveness.

To the true believers, for whom a belief in deity is the bedrock of religion, the degeneration of Wicca into sitcom fodder is a tragedy. Yet these believers cannot abandon the faith, even as they deplore some of the fake-faithful who are now swelling the ranks, drawn to us because they've bought the false images, not the religious tenets.

It's time to make a distinction between true *spirituality* and *religion*. Religion is the rituals we devise in our attempt to honor the gods, the ceremonies that help us through our life passages and good or difficult times.

Spirituality is what comes to us unbidden. It is the revelation that comes out of nowhere; the sudden strength that helps us survive the unbearable or teaches us something that changes us forever. It comes in big ways and small increments, but we can never mistake it for anything else. These are the real Mysteries, the communication between divinity and humanity, the ultimate goal of religion.

Many high priestesses and high priests have never understood the Mysteries. You can tell by their insistence on form and function and not a word on personal spiritual transformation. I doubt that many televangelists and big-name preachers have had these revelations either, since when they claim to have had them, the "revelation from God" always had to do with church membership, collecting money, or the importance of conforming to religious doctrine.

Genuine spirituality does not require you to "give over your life" or sit out in the desert waiting for enlightenment. It comes to you when it comes, in the course of everyday living. If you're looking for the real secret of Wicca, that's where you'll find it.

No matter how Wicca started out, amid a messy morass of half-truths, borrowed rituals, and invented history, the fact is that what is emerging is a religion that speaks to people, that satisfies something within us that longs for spiritual assurance.

Despite our loudly proclaimed disdain for "organized religion," almost all Wiccans are looking for some group identification, some shared philosophy that binds us all together, a set of rituals and principles that support us through life passages both joyful and painful. We need that stuff. Everyone does. If we didn't need it, half my mail wouldn't be from people looking for covens. (The other half is from people looking for help on term papers about the Salem trials—and just so you know, my answer is: *Read a history book.*)

Frankly, you can't get away from "organized religion": Religion is by definition organized. It's the system of rules and ritual we use to honor whatever gods we believe in, even if that system is practiced by only one person. It can be as simple as remembering the gods once a day; it can be as elaborate as the ceremonies surrounding the anointing of a new pope. *Religion* is man-made; *spirituality* is a touch from the divine.

Wicca is just about as organized as any other religion. Attend a Circle in Los Angeles, New York, Nashville, or Rome (Italy *or* Georgia) and you're going to find that the basic structure is more or less the same: Cast the Circle, call the Elements, invoke the gods, share the chalice, thank the gods, dismiss the energies, open the Circle.

What delights me about Wicca is that the Circle can be a simple fifteen-minute silent meditation or a two-hour extravaganza with a choreographer and special fire effects, with the high priestess in ruby slippers descending from the ceiling in a cloud—but *if the intent is devout and sincere,* the end result is still the same. People are going to feel better when they leave.

That's religion for you.

If you're a new Wiccan, be advised that this isn't another "how to do it" beginner book, although there's some basic information in some cases. I'm assuming that you've read a few books or have had some practical exposure to Wicca, and you know some of the lingo. You're not going to learn how to cast a Circle or how to do spells. I want to give you some real info and advice to help you separate some of the myths about our religion from the truth. There's a lot of Wiccan revisionism going on right now, and that's a *good* thing, but it can get confusing. Here you thought that the statement, "Wicca is a pre-Christian religion going back to the ancient worship of a Great Mother Goddess" was absolutely true. Now, reexamining the evidence, we're not so sure.

You'll also discover the Fifteen Things Everybody Knows but You, something I wish someone had told *me* when I started out. I can't count the number of gatherings I went to where I stood by in total confusion, thinking, *Is it refreshment time yet?* (Actually, there are some Circles where I still do this.)

If you want to be taken seriously right off the bat, check out the Three Things That Definitely Mark You as a Beginner (see chapter 11). Say any one of these three things and people are going to chuckle. They may not do it to your face, but they'll do it.

There's also some really unpleasant stuff masquerading as Wicca, and some other unpleasant stuff that's actually perpetrated by Wiccans who should know better. You might as well know about it now rather than later, to avoid disappointment or worse.

If you've been around for a while, practicing either solitary or with a group, you're probably reassessing many of the ideas you've been taught. Most of us, who really care about the religion and want it to thrive, are having to do this—even if it means tossing some of our most cherished "facts."

We're not the first religion that's been through this: We're just the newest. Even Christian historians are still arguing over what actually happened during the lifetime of Jesus and how the gospels were revised and rewritten hundreds of years after the poor guy died for upsetting the system. They've had two thousand years to figure this out, and they're still at it, so I wouldn't feel too badly about Wiccan revisionism.

Frankly, I find it awesome that, in our lifetime, a new religion is being established. And instead of waiting hundreds of years to shake off our misconceptions and mistakes, we're doing it only fifty years, more or less, after its introduction.

Wicca has now had time to grow, and Wiccans have done more research into our religious roots. We have our true believers, people who have been quietly practicing their religion in dignified, private, meaningful rituals that support them through their days, in good times and in not so good. It gives them strength, comfort, and compassion. It doesn't get them on Jerry Springer or in those Halloween specials that crop up on TV every October, and they'd be appalled if it did. They're the backbone of the religion, but as far as the media is concerned, they're overshadowed by the black-robes-and-pounds-o'-jewelry crowd, the Role-Playing Gamers, the Witch Queens of the World, the Goth-wannabe kids, and the black-lipstick and gaudy-tats junkies. Unfortunately, these are the people who end up on the TV talk shows, selected precisely because they fit the producers' image of what a "real" Witch should be: *bizarre*. How many of these shows have you seen that include a Wiccan priestess, a rabbi, and a bishop discussing serious religious and social issues?

That's changing, as serious Wiccans refuse to go along with this silliness. And lest you think that I'm Miss Religious Purity, there's an interview on the Travel Channel that I really wish I could do over—this time without the black velvet robes and the unfortunate earrings.

People ask me if I'm a practicing Wiccan and I tell 'em that I don't need any more practice, I've about got it down by now. But you know what? We never stop learning. We'll never know for sure what went on in the mind of Gerald Gardner, whether the New Forest Coven was all he said it was, or how much was inherited and how much invented. We'll never know for sure exactly what the Druids did on May Day, or what went on during the Bacchic Mysteries. We don't know if there really was a woman-dominated, idyllic culture at Catal Hayuk or other anthropological sites (although, from recent analysis, all signs point to a big *no*). If we're waiting to know everything, we're gonna wait a hell of a long time.

So . . . we take what's good, we use what's working, and we keep uncovering the real Wicca, rather than the Disney version.

But we can't be afraid to look at what we're doing wrong, as well as what's going right. For a long time, Wiccans have had the world's thickest blinders when it came to our religion. We read and accepted only what was complimentary to our ideas and rebuked any criticism as "anti-Wiccan." We refused to admit that any of our history was shaky, or that anyone in Wicca could be less than honest. I can't count the number of times I've heard people say, "Oh, but he can't be guilty of that, he's *Wiccan!*"

Worse is the fact that Wiccans—experienced practitioners as well as newcomers—have fallen for some unbelievable scams and unconscionable behavior that they would never have tolerated from an outsider. We like to disparage the people who believe every word that a televangelist utters, and then we submit ourselves to the whim of some bogus "Lady Somebody" who tells us that the way to true enlightenment is to scrub her kitchen floor, or "Lord Whatever" who requires his students to work long hours at his business for sweatshop wages.

And whether we like it or not, there are plenty of Wiccans who are just in it for the money, or the power over other people, or the quick fix of fame. Some are simply desperate for some kind of attention.

But the worst is what we sometimes do to ourselves and the dignity of our religion when we decide to become the media's bitch. When we let the image of "Witch" be determined by leftover ideas from the Inquisition and religious fanatics. When we protest "stereotypes" while dressed like an Edgar Allan Poe reject.

Forewarned is forearmed, they say, and they're right. Time to take a look at the good, the bad, and the nasty; at what we can change and what needs to go. There are plenty of things in this book that I wish didn't go on. But since we're being honest here, you might as well get all the dirt as well as the good stuff. Witches are a gossipy bunch anyway, like all small, insular groups—and if you think we're the only ones, just attend the local Church Ladies' Bean Supper on Wednesday nights and listen to all the slander being slung.

You might think that this book has too much information about Salem and the Witches here, but Salem is where I live and practice, so I know it better than other places. And the town has become a microcosm, combining some of the best and the worst about Wicca. Many, many Wiccans and Pagans come here every year, looking for some idealized Wiccan Heaven that will welcome them with no questions asked and solve all their problems. Many burn out fast, after going from group to group, expecting the Salem community to give while they do nothing but take. But some of them bring good experience with them, energizing the community. As it is, Salem isn't much different from any other town, except that we have more tacky tourist traps than anyplace east of Las Vegas.

This book represents my opinions and observations over an involvement with Wicca since the late 1970s. It's a very personal book for me. Although I now follow a path that's more Pagan than mainstream Wiccan, it's still my religion, and I want to see it grow into a mature, nurturing religion that is respected by society. I don't care if other religions agree with us, so long as they respect our rights to hold our views. I'd like to see the time come when Wiccan kids aren't ridiculed, when Wiccans aren't regarded as flaky, and when we can openly own up to being Wiccans without the fear of discrimination or, more often, the slightly amused and condescending attitudes that we have to put up with today.

In order for that to happen, I think that we have to be willing to cast off a lot of our old ideas, even some that we most cherish, if it helps us get to the truth. We keep insisting on the ancient origins of our religions, but most of us don't want to examine that claim too closely: For every scholar who agrees with us, there's another one who doesn't. I'm not attempting to solve that argument here; I'd just like to make Wiccans aware of the arguments, and the fact that we need not be afraid of the outcome. Even if we could point to some exact truth about ancient matriarchal Goddess-worshiping societies, what difference would it really make? And if there never was one, what difference would *that* make? Frankly, not a whole lot: We're going to believe what we believe no matter what, if it makes us happy.

But this insistence on our antiquity is becoming a real burden. Combing through the past for any little fragment that supports our theories takes up time and energy that we should be devoting to the present and future of the religion. Insistence on "lineage" as any proof of sincere belief or enlightenment or power is just as useless.

In the end it comes down to faith, just like every other religion. But it would be good for us if we could accept that any claims to antiquity are irrelevant. It's what the religion is doing for us here and now that really matters.

And what we're willing to do for the religion to shape its future.

2

What Flavor Are You?

A Witch? A Wiccan? A Pagan? What's the Difference?

What makes a Witch, a Wiccan, or a Pagan? Can just calling your-self a Wiccan make you one? When I started writing this book, I was convinced that after all these years as a Witch, a teacher, and a writer, I definitely knew the answer to that question.

But in the past few years, Wicca has changed, and—I believe—for the better.

For one thing, Wicca has become spectacularly visible. Lots of Witches, sick of stuffing their pentagrams inside their shirts and suffering in silence while some uninformed jerk on the evening news equates Wicca with devil-worshipin' baby-eatin' black-mass-practicin' flakewits, have decided that we have just as much right to worship openly as everyone else. When Wiccans are seen actively living our religion instead of just talking about it in vague terms, people sometimes are interested enough to seek out more information. Some decide that Wicca answers their questions and satisfies their spiritual longings.

And then there are the newer movies and TV shows about

Witchcraft and Wicca, and if you think I'm going to knock those shows, you're wrong. Okay, the movie *The Craft* and the TV shows *Charmed, Sabrina the Teenage Witch,* and cute little Willow, Buffy's friend, are not accurate portrayals of Wicca, and they include some really silly stuff about magic. But *at least* they're not equating Witchcraft with evil. Quite the opposite. *Buffy the Vampire Slayer* has established that Willow and Tara worship a Goddess and they use their powers to combat the villains. Although, at this writing, Willow's gotten into some pretty heavy manipulative magic and is paying the price for it. (Even so, there are a lot of Wiccans who would agree with that principle.) I really miss Cybill Shepard's sitcom: It showed a modern, active woman who had made a place in her life for the Maiden, Mother, and Crone; one of the characters even kept a shrine to Kali in her bedroom.

Many Wiccans hate these shows because the MTV-style "witches" with the perfect hair and makeup are able to do things like point their fingers and conjure stuff or throw energy fireballs at bad guys. Oh, come on . . . you *know* that we wish we could do that stuff, just like we wish we'd gone to Hogwarts—so don't even bother denying it.

What these movies and TV shows *have* done is interest young people in Wicca. And if the kids are serious, they seek out books and do some research into the religion. I've heard older Wiccans bitching and moaning about the fact that the kids are just playing around, that they won't stick to the religion in the long run. Well, so what? At least they'll have learned something, and any kid who's read a couple of books on Wicca will have grasped the basic ideas. One more accurately informed person in the world isn't a bad thing. And as for staying in the religion: How many people have left their original religions to come to Wicca or to other religions? Conversion is the building block of many a mainstream religion. In fact, ours is one of the few religions that doesn't actively seek converts.

All of this has brought many previously secretive Wiccans out of the shadows, and has brought newcomers into the religion.

People are suddenly finding out that the nice old lady next door or the cute young couple down the block or the guy in the next office are Wiccans. And they look just the same as everyone else! They had no *idea!*

Some people who are having to deal with it are us old-line Wiccans. The religion is changing. For one thing, it's attracting a lot of young people, and that's something we should treasure.

What Defines a Witch?

People have been arguing about this for years, and no one has yet reached a conclusion that's satisfactory to all. So naturally, with the bravado of the foolhardy, I've decided to give it a shot. For the purposes of this book, let's say that the following general and brief definitions are true, especially for Wiccans.

Wiccans. Strictly speaking, Wicca is a religious path. The belief system was first set down publicly by Gerald Gardner in his book *Witchcraft Today*, published in the 1950s. It's a sure thing that he attached the name to the practice. Whether he made it all up, or whether it was passed down to him by an old coven practicing ancient rites, or whether it was a combination of traditional material and new ideas augmented by Gardner is something we'll never know for sure. People have been delving into this question for years, and entire books pro and con have been written purporting to have the real lowdown on Gardner.

The debate can continue forever, but by now it makes no difference where the religion came from, because it's here to stay. *Every* religion was made up by *somebody,* and every one of them claim that they were founded because some deity or some deity's sales rep (usually referred to as a *prophet*) said that system was the real deal. Some religions may be older than others, but that doesn't make them any more or less valid than others.

Wiccan hard-liners say that you can't really be a Wiccan unless you've been trained and initiated into a coven with a direct line back to Gardner. There's some justification for this. Since much of the information, ritual, and philosophy of Gardnerian Wicca is taught only to those who are initiated into the line, and those people take an oath never to reveal that information, you'll just never know what the Gardnerians know unless you become one of them. This is despite the accusations that several people have broken their oaths and published true Gardnerian material.

Like it or not, however, the term *Wiccan* has been vastly expanded to include almost anyone who practices a polytheistic religion based (however loosely) on Gardner's teachings, who believes in a creator-goddess and a god, and who follows the Wiccan Rede and the Threefold Law. In some cases, being Wiccan doesn't even have to include all these elements, and it frequently includes more. It's come to the point where if you call yourself a Wiccan, then you are one.

Gardnerians and some others deplore all this "do-it-yourself" Wicca, but they're just going to have to live with it. (Don't they say that they're supposed to "suffer to learn," anyway?) It's too late now to hold back the tide.

So let's say that generally, Wiccans are people for whom Wicca is a religion, usually some derivative of the principles set out in the 1950s by Gerald Gardner. They follow the Wiccan Rede, or rule ("Harm none and do what you will"), and the Threefold Law of Karma ("Everything that you do comes back to you threefold"), and usually, but not always, practice magic. When they do practice magic, it is usually nonmanipulative: no curses, personal bindings, or interfering with anyone's free will.

Wiccans claim, as did Gardner, that Wicca is a survival of a Pagan religion. This comes from a theory (and it is only a theory, since there's no solid proof) advanced by Egyptologist Margaret Murray. Murray's theory, in short, says, "The evidence proves that underlying the Christian religion was a cult practiced by many classes of the community, chiefly, however, by the more ignorant or those in the less thickly inhabited parts of the country. It can be traced back to pre-Christian times and appears to be the ancient religion of western Europe."*

Um . . . well . . . the evidence doesn't exactly prove that at all. Maybe the theory is bolstered by Murray's own evidence, which was selective, as is the evidence of many writers since, who have based their own work on Murray's in an attempt to prove that Wicca is the remnant of an ancient matriarchal religion or society. This was especially true in the late 1960s and early 1970s, during the height of the women's movement: The idea was that both the movement and Wicca would have gained historical validity if this connection could have been proven beyond a doubt. Women *wanted* this to be true, with such a passion that dissenting evidence was often overlooked or shunted aside as irrelevant.

There's no doubt that the idea of witches existed in early times—the Romans had charms against them—but Pagan cults were very individualistic. There were hundreds of tribes throughout Europe, and each tribe had its own gods and practices specific to those gods. There was no "ancient religion of western Europe" in any sense of a single widespread religion with similar practices. And many of those individual practices were assimilated into those of that Borg of the ancient world, the Roman Empire. The Romans maintained a live-and-let-live attitude toward religion, but eventually the tribes of Europe were "civilized," which included a gradual transition into the Roman way of living, including religion. That's not to say that Pagan *ideas* didn't survive: they certainly did. Christianity owes almost as much to Paganism as it does to Judaism.

Historian Richard Cavendish says, "In England, one of the last bastions of Paganism in western Europe, there is no evidence that Pagan cults survived later than the time of Canute, who died in 1035."†

---

*Margaret Murray, *The Witch-Cult in Western Europe,* Clarendon Press, Oxford, 1921.

†Richard Cavendish, *The Black Arts,* Perigee Books, New York, 1967.

Wiccans are almost always polytheistic: They believe in many gods, even though they may speak only of "the Goddess" and "the God." This belief in many gods, and in a female creator or co-creator, is in opposition to the belief of most mainstream religions, especially Christianity, which demands a belief in Jehovah as the one true God, and a belief that Jesus was the Messiah and the son of that God. Because of this, there can be no such thing as a "Christian Wiccan" since the most important and inflexible beliefs of the two religions are incompatible.

I'm always getting asked if you can be a Wiccan and still be a Christian. I usually ask the person: "Why aren't you asking your priest or pastor that question?" Probably because he or she can anticipate the answer. *My* answer is no. How can you practice two religions at once, one of which requires that you deny all others? You'd be dishonoring both of them.

Many Wiccans refer to themselves as Witches, using the terms interchangeably, and you're going to see me do it in this book, too. Old habits die hard.

Witches practice magic but do not necessarily follow the Wiccan Rede or the Threefold Law. Witchcraft is not always a religious path; therefore, Christians can practice magic and call themselves Witches, and many of them do. Some Witches are *hereditary:* that is, they were born into Witch families or inherited the practice from a relative. This claim used to be a source of much amusement in the Witch community because every other Witch claimed a generations-old tradition, almost always passed on by Granny and kept a big secret from the rest of the family. The good news is that as Wicca and Witchcraft have been becoming more prominent in the United States since the 1960s, a lot of those early practitioners have raised their kids as Wiccans or Witches, and second- and third-generation Witches and Wiccans are not unusual.

In the past, some Witches called themselves Wiccans or Pagans simply to avoid the stereotypes that the word *Witch* triggers. This practice is waning, however, as the differences between Wiccans and Witches come more into focus, and more people are able to speak publicly about their beliefs. Most Witches feel strongly about *not* referring to themselves as Wiccans.

Pagans have it somewhat easier than Wiccans or Witches. In the first place, everyone has a pretty good idea of what a Pagan is: somebody who's not a Christian, Jew, Muslim, or any other follower of Big Religion, but still believes in a god or gods. Pagans don't usually take the heat that attaches to Wiccans and Witches: Tell somebody that you're a Pagan, and they think you're kidding, or that you just like to party. Tell them you're a heathen and they'll laugh even harder. This makes it pretty difficult to garner any respect for your beliefs, but it also leaves you less open to discrimination. The drawback here is that people assume you're an atheist. Which, when you consider how many gods Pagans honor, is ludicrous.

Also, Pagans trying to reconstruct religious rituals of the past have it easier than Wiccans, depending on the kind of Paganism they practice. For instance, Pagans who follow the *Religio Romana,* the state religion of ancient Rome, have plenty of documented sources to draw from. Finding and reconstructing ritual isn't the problem; the problem is adapting religious rituals to the modern world. These days, it's plenty tough to sacrifice a white bull to Mithras, no matter how strongly you believe. Unless, of course, you can get a job in the local meatpacking industry as a slaughterhouse worker: Every time a white bull comes along, you could just yell, "This one's for Mithras!" and relax in the knowledge that you've done your religious duty.

Pagans generally believe in many gods. There are exceptions, however. For example, some followers of the Egyptian sun god Aten or Amon, if they're following the strict historical belief system set down by the Pharaoh Akhenaton, consider him the one true God.

Ceremonial magicians are a class unto themselves. They practice "high magic" as opposed to "low magic" or the folk magic and spellwork that most of us do. These are *serious* magical people. They don't do "spells," they do "workings," and there's a big difference. Ceremonial magic workings require great discipline and can take up to a year to complete. Everything relating to the working must be done perfectly—or you have to start over from the beginning. In this way, ceremonial magic shares quite a few traits with its predecessor, alchemy. In today's world, the looser definition of ceremonial magic also includes Rosicrucians, followers of the new version of the Golden Dawn, Kabbalists, and the followers of Aleister Crowley in groups like the O.T.O. and the various Thelemites.

Also, real ceremonial magicians are rare, precisely because of the self-discipline and exacting requirements. Particularly in America, the "have-it-all, have-it-now, short-attention-span, instant-results" lifestyle isn't compatible with long-term workings. Also, to give us credit, Americans just don't have a history of ceremonial magic and alchemy, the way the Brits and Europeans do. We didn't have kings to finance it, for one thing. Although I used to drive by a big industrial building in Connecticut that had a corporate-type sign that said: ALCHEMISTS. Beside the building were huge hills of rusted iron and metal. I never found out what *that* was all about.

For this book, we won't be getting into ceremonial magic, except the parts that have spilled over into Wicca. But as we'll see in chapter 6, on Traditions, that's a lot.

Why I Don't Believe in Witches: A Very Compressed Historical Overview

The most prevalent definition of a witch (small w) comes from the thirteenth to the eighteenth centuries and was used as a catchall to rid the church of heretics. The church defined a witch as a devil worshiper who sold his or her soul, drank blood, flew through the air to blasphemous meetings and disgusting orgies, killed babies, and worked evil magic against "good Christian people."

Fortunately those witches never existed. So, I don't believe in them.

And where did the church get these ideas? Well, you can't blame the Christians for it, although most Wiccans would love to. Oddly enough, many of the old, familiar lies about witches originated in Paganism, and they were applied to Christians. To get an idea of how old the fallacies are, you'd have to go pretty far back, but let's start in Rome during the early imperial period. Some of these slanderous ideas probably date from an earlier time, but the most famous application of them is by Romans to Christians.

Rome provided a fairly lenient atmosphere in terms of religious freedom. Because it had conquered pretty much the known world at the time, the city was packed with foreigners: imported slaves captured in military campaigns, diplomats from the provinces ruled by Rome or granted "Friend and Ally" status, craftsmen and tradesmen who had come to Rome to make their fortunes, freed slaves who had done very well for themselves. Lots of religious preferences, lots of strange cults. Rome didn't mind if, for example, the adherents of the Great Mother, Cybele, built a temple and imported their eunuch priests to Rome. And Romans who were drawn to this worship were free to join up. (But not to join the testicle-choppin' priesthood, that was for sure, since Roman law frowned on anything that hindered procreation—you were supposed to produce sons for the senate if you were a patrician, or for the legions if you were of the less exalted class.)

The Senate and People of Rome didn't mind what gods you worshiped in private, as long as you granted respect and honor in public to the official state religion, the *Religio Romana,* which honored the old gods of Rome. Incidentally, the *Religio Romana* is making a comeback in a big way because of the efforts of groups like Nova Roma and various Roman reenactor organizations.

The Christians had a big problem with Roman religion. That is to say, they didn't believe in it. That wasn't *great,* but it wasn't *illegal,* not as long as they turned out for the official state religious rites. Unfortunately they didn't. Plus, they advocated that no one else should believe in the official religion, either, because it was a false religion. They encouraged people to leave the established religion and join theirs. They preached that everyone, slave or emperor, was of the same class, equal in God's eyes. That was another problem: They said that there was only one God, and he *wasn't* any of the gods worshiped in Rome. Their idea about a Messiah—adapted from Hebrew mythology—was that the Messiah had already come (and gone, by that time) and they knew who he was: a Nazarene ex-carpenter named Joshua bar Joseph, aka Jesus. He was going to lead people away from the "false religion" of Rome and overthrow the empire. A little detail like his having been crucified was not a problem, because he was the son of the true God and had risen from the dead.

Uh-oh. Anyone with three working brain cells could see that this attitude was not going to win the Christians any friends among the ruling class. And the Christians were very vocal about their beliefs, too, encouraging what the government interpreted as insurrection. The Romans, usually so relaxed about religion, finally outlawed the Christian cult because it threatened the stability of the government. To understand this, you must first understand that religion and the state were inseparable in Rome. Threaten one, and you threatened both. And these Christians were just so annoying. Some Christian slaves captured in Judea and elsewhere were making trouble in Rome by converting their masters and mistresses. This didn't happen often, but it happened often enough to be worrying.

Clearly, a little disinformation was called for.

Rumors began to circulate about the abominable, disgusting practices of this new cult. It was said that they held secret sexual rites that degenerated into debauches, that they killed children for sacrifices to a strange god, that they drank blood and practiced cannibalism, eating and drinking the body and blood of their god. More disgusting: They kept pieces of dead people around as relics. Eeeuuww.

Sound familiar? Does the later Inquisition spring to mind? These were exactly the same charges that the Christians later used against the Jews, the Cathars, the Knights Templar, and any others who dared question the authority of the church. They're also the same arguments that fundamentalists use against Wiccans. This is another classic case of the abused learning to abuse others.

Emperor Nero hated Christians so much that he had them crucified and set on fire in his garden to provide light for festive evening parties. But . . . that was Nero, and he was young, rich, and insane. Other emperors simply settled for execution *ad bestias,* meaning that the offenders were killed by animals in the arena, which was a standard execution method for crimes against the state. So was crucifixion.

Christianity's opportunity to make it as a big-time religion came with the Emperor Constantine, who had some kind of vision before battle and decided to convert. The vision was of a cross and the words *In this sign you will conquer.* Or so he claimed. Whether he really believed, or whether he could see that it was politically expedient, given the large numbers of Christians coming into positions of power, is still debated.

Like them or not, the Romans spread civilization and order through all the provinces they ruled. They'd conquer your country, stick a good Roman boy in as provincial governor, lay down some laws, build you some nice roads and plumbing, and you'd send your grateful tax bucks to Rome and the legions wouldn't bother you any more. In fact, they'd protect you against your enemies. Also, the Romans were big on education, at least in reading and writing in Latin and Greek. The Romans honestly could not see why anyone would object to this system.

Eventually all that changed. In Europe, the gradual fall of the civilized Roman Empire made way for the Dark Ages, fueled by a new religion of fear, during which learning was reserved for the priests. Even the majority of the upper classes couldn't read or write. Pagan religion was dead.

A great blanket of superstition fueled by dread of hellfire

smothered any remnants of education or enlightenment. This was bad for the people, but just dandy for the church. It was the perfect atmosphere to establish control over society and politics. It was, as Hitler would later proclaim of his own hostile takeover, a "New World Order." Oddly enough, a phrase most recently used by televangelist Pat Robertson and ex-president and CIA head George Bush the First. Hmm.

And if anyone threatened that order in any way, especially by questioning the superstitions that formed the bedrock of the church, the Christians recalled a really effective way to silence them. Remember those old rumors that the Romans dredged up to discredit the early Christians? Ooooh, those were nasty! Let's apply them to those heretics who are giving us a hard time!

But you can't just kill people's friends, neighbors, and relatives. First, you have to create fear of them. Tell the people that these church-hating troublemakers are imbued with supernatural powers because they're in cahoots with the Devil. This is a great tactic: When any natural disaster comes along, or Farmer Theodoric's cow dies, or the crops fail, it's because of the magical actions of these godless people.

Pretty soon you don't have to even bother to hunt for the heretics, because their terrified neighbors are more than happy to turn them in. After all, didn't the church quote Bible verses to prove that these people were evil? And wasn't it your duty, as a God-fearing, Jesus-loving, tithe-paying churchgoer, to denounce them? Selling your enemies out to be executed was not only personally gratifying, it gave you a nice warm glow of knowing that you were making God happy. Doing the right thing.

The Cathars

The witch hunts didn't start out specifically to find witches. The seeds were planted when the church was faced with popular and growing heretical sects. The most rabid persecutions were aimed at a sect called the Cathars, which had challenged the basics of church belief. If you're going to understand the ideas that stirred up the church against witches, you're going to have to understand some things about the Cathars. Catharism started in northern Italy in the early eleventh century, and by the twelfth it was really taking hold in the south of France, around Carcassonne and Rennes-le-Château in the Languedoc region (for all you conspiracy and/or treasure-hunting fans, this is a significant location*), and had become entrenched with the nobility. To the church's horror, the movement was spreading all the way to Germany. Briefly, the Cathars believed that the Old Testament God was, in fact, Satan. Since they didn't believe in sex—to make babies was to obey Jehovah (actually Satan, remember) and his command to be fruitful and multiply—it's hard to see how this group made such a big hit in France. They rejected sex, violence, lying, owning property, and taking oaths. Plus, they were (gasp!) *vegetarians*. So much for French cuisine.

But wait! Those prohibitions were only for the high-ranking adepts, called Perfects. And there weren't all that many of those, understandably. All the *lower ranks* of Cathars were free from these rules. Since they were already enslaved by the Devil, they were traveling on the highway to hell anyway, so they could eat, drink, be merry, and—most important—screw around. Marriage, however, was out. To marry was to produce children, and to produce children was a sin. However, any sexual activity that *didn't* produce children was okay. Now you can begin to see why Catharism was hot. The Cathars believed that the church of Rome was the Devil's tool (don't forget: Jehovah = Satan) and rejected its teachings as sinful.

This led, inevitably, to "You're the Devil's church!" "No, *you* are!" "No, YOU are!" and it was clear that only the last man standing was going to settle this one.

Since the church of Rome had a vast army, most people were

---

*Michael Baigent, Richard Leigh, Henry Lincoln, *Holy Blood, Holy Grail*, Delacort Press, New York, 1982. The treasure of the Cathars and the bloodline of Jesus is one of the world's most intriguing and complicated mysteries, and I'm *not* getting into it here, but I wish I could.

calling their bookies to place a big one on the once-and-future Catholics. Sure enough, the church got together a crusade and the Cathars were shortly knockin' on heaven's door. Or somebody's.

What's important here are the charges leveled against the Cathars: worshiping the Devil in the form of a goat or cat; stealing children; eating babies; flying through the air to "synagogues" (the word that came to be associated with witch meetings and continued to be applied during the witch hysteria, from Revelation 2:9) by means of broomsticks and flying ointment. The same charges applied to a sect called the Waldensians or Vaudois, which was also accused of sorcery.*

Every time the church purged itself of rebellious sects, it used the excuse of heresy, and the charges leveled against these sects became more and more fanciful, comprising what we know now as the basics of diabolism. There were a lot of sects; the best known at the time were Luciferans (guess where the concepts of the black mass came from?) and the Knights Templar. The Templars weren't even a sect: They were an arm of the church that had become too rich, too powerful, and too independent. The charges against them were similar to the charges against the other groups.

Even though the old charges of evil and debauchery were hanging around, the church still needed some kind of scapegoat to personify them all. And that scapegoat was the witch. The Bible even provided a good excuse to kill witches, provided you were willing to overlook the original translation of Ezekiel, which actually read, "Thou shalt not allow a poisoner to live among you."

Most people conveniently blame "the Inquisition" for the witch trials, and certainly they were the most infamous. But the first known witch trials were in France in 1245 in Toulouse, a Cathar stronghold. A hundred years later, in the same area, we have ac-

---

*Cavendish says that the practice of *vauderie,* sorcery, is the root of the word *voodoo,* which is likely, since many slaves practicing their tribal religion were imported to French colonies. When blacks rose up in revolt in eighteenth-century Haiti, many ex-slaves fled to Louisiana, where the religion mutated into modern voodoo.

counts of the "witches' Sabbath." Apparently, Catharism was slow to die out completely, and probably had its own "survival" in secret.

A hundred years after the massacre of the Cathars, in 1435, a sensational book appeared in Germany, written by the Inquisitor John Nider. The *Formicarium* was a handy, five-volume list of all the possible sins against religion, but the really good stuff was in the last volume, a treatise on the crimes of witches. Here you could find the old tried-and-true accusations of fortune-telling, second sight, the power to cause disease and death, shape-shifting, raising storms, debauchery . . . and killing and eating babies.

It's interesting to note that, prior to the fifteenth and sixteenth centuries in Germany, belief in witchcraft was against the law. But as the church took hold, it brought fear and an unhealthy superstition with it. Anthropologist Lewis Spence says, "It may be truly said that the Holy Fathers and the Inquisition first systemized and formulated Black Magic."*

But it was up to two psychotic monks, Heinrich Kramer and Jacob Sprenger, to set down the basic guide to witch hunting, giving a focus to the hysteria. They devised a mishmash of superstition and outright lies, and revised the ancient Roman charges leveled against the Christians, this time describing witches. The resulting book, *Malleus Maleficarum,* was published and approved by papal bull (the pope's official "okey-dokey") in 1484, and the church believed every word of it. For greater ease and convenience in torturing innocent people, the book included a handy list of the hallmarks of witches, which were: They worked evil magic to hurt people, had supernatural powers, and had made a deal with Satan, whom they worshiped with disgusting evil rituals that included sexual deviance and—surprise!—killing and eating babies. (*Useful note:* If you're planning a social insurrection, you can't go wrong by scaring people with the old "These people are a threat to our *children!*" line. Even the most neglectful parent will suddenly

---

*Lewis Spence, *The Encyclopedia of the Occult,* Bracken Books, London, 1988.

become more defensive than a mother tiger when hearing this, especially if it's sprinkled with religious overtones.) Every disgusting accusation that had been leveled against the heretic sects was tossed into the *Malleus*.

If you asked people whether or not they were witches, they'd deny it. Better devise a few tests—the more painful, the better—to get at the truth. And the only acceptable truth was: Yes, I'm a witch and I did all that you said and more. Victims were encouraged to describe "more" in gruesome detail, which was added to the records and the resulting folklore. It's interesting to ponder how long it takes until "rumor" turns into folklore, but it happens all the time.

Some of our more revolting ideas about witches come from the confessions of the accused, most of which were obtained under torture, and the details of which were suggested by the examiners' questions. These "confessions" were actually prewritten documents; all the accused witch had to do was sign. Still, the confessions of one Isobel Gowdie provide both the usual atrocities, and a few unique features, so let's take a closer look at her.

Isobel Gowdie, Psycho and Witch

Perhaps no accused witch is more responsible for the bulk of sheer nonsense about witches than Isobel Gowdie, tried for witchcraft in Scotland in 1662. In Isobel, the witch hunters had a confirmation of everything they believed about diabolism.

Scotland was certainly rife with wicked-witch lore. Robert Burns's *Tale of Tam o' Shanter*, written in 1791, long after the witch hunts, describes old Scottish legends of witches gathering at Candlemas, Beltane, and Hallow's Eve, arriving from all over the world in eggshell boats and on goblin horses that rode through the air.

In the early 1600s, Scotland was a hotbed of diabolic activity, according to the clergy and the king. Talk about "uneasy rests the head that wears the crown"! James I saw witches and demons lurking in every shadow, and it drove him nuts.

The Scottish imagination has always been rather grim; under

James's influence, it became positively morbid. James, a natural neurotic, had spent quite a bit of time on the Continent, especially in France—teeming with witch hysteria at the time he was there—and he had become obsessed with witchcraft and witches.

When he was returning home, his ship was caught in a storm and nearly lost. Irrational with fear, James blamed witches for raising the storm. (Later, his torture squad managed to get a confession from a "witch" pertaining to this very thing. That confession snowballed into the prosecution of over seventy people, including the powerful Earl of Bothwell.)

Back home, James proceeded to write his treatise on witchcraft and diabolism, *Daemonologie,* published in 1599, which became a supporting text for witch hunters. It's safe to say that James was highly influenced by the work of Kramer and Sprenger, whose ideas had become the definitive thinking on European witchcraft.

The torturers didn't even have to touch Isobel to get a confession out of her. She volunteered. The woman was obviously mentally ill, and just as obviously believed all the delusions to which she confessed. She confirmed all the nasty practices that were suggested to her, and added some salacious embroideries of her own. Between April and May 1662, she gave four separate sensational confessions, in which she either confirmed the prevailing beliefs about witches or added her demented details to the witch hunters' arsenals. A great deal of what we now associate with diabolic witchcraft was either confirmed by or first surfaced in Isobel's confessions: that witches group together in covens of thirteen, fly on broomsticks to the Sabbats, take a "witch name" in a satanic baptism, bear Devil's marks on their bodies, shape-shift, and consort with demons in the form of familiars. Riding to witch meetings wasn't a new idea. As early as the ninth century, the church made reference to women riding on beasts to attend meetings. The Council of Treves in 1310 condemned women who believed themselves to ride through the air with Diana, Herodiana, or Herodias.

The most astonishing of Isobel's confessions was also the one in which the witch hunters were most interested: her description of sex with the Horndog of Hades himself, Satan.

> And within a few days, he came to me, in the New Wards of Inshoch, and there had carnal copulation with me. He was a very huge, black, rough man, very cold; and I found his nature [*semen*] within me all cold as spring well water. He will lie all heavy upon us, when he has carnal dealing with us, like a sack of barley malt. His member is exceedingly great and long; no man's member is so long and big as his. He would be among us like a stud horse among mares.
>
> The youngest and lustiest women will have very great pleasure in their carnal copulation with him, yea much more than with their own husbands; and they will have an exceedingly great desire for it with him, as much as he can give them and more, and never think shame of it. He is abler for us that way than any man can be (Alas! that I should compare him to any man!) only he is heavy like a sack of barley malt; a huge nature [*emission*], very cold as ice.

Obviously, hootchie-mama Isobel badly needed a guy—or a vibrator. To the popular imagination, Isobel was the seventeenth-century combination of Stephen King and Larry Flynt. The sexual element was exactly the sort of thing that kept the witch hunters and the population in general panting for more. In a sexually repressed society, this was hot stuff beyond imagination, and the word spread fast.

The most important thing was that someone *willingly* confessed to everything that the witch hunters wanted to hear, and more besides. As far as they were concerned, this was absolute proof that the practice of witchcraft as outlined by Sprenger and Kramer was true. Having anything at all to do with the Devil was bad enough; having sex with the guy really put you beyond all salvation. Isobel's confessions, widely circulated, formed the conventional wisdom of what constituted the practice of witchcraft.

What makes her confessions even more unlikely is that Isobel was a Scottish peasant, and her descriptions of witches' Sabbats and practices sound definitely French and German. Exactly as King James described them in *Daemonologie*. What a coincidence!

You'd think that in a more enlightened time, her pitiful confessions would be looked upon as exactly what they were: the effusions of a diseased mind, its delusions fueled by some not-so-subtle suggestions by the witch hunters. But in the twentieth century, Isobel's sad meanderings were given further credence by two scholars, Montague Summers and Margaret Murray. Both of them picked up the confessions to bolster their own agendas. Summers (whose religious and academic credentials were dubious, and who believed everything he read, no matter how incredible) endorsed them as essentially true. Murray used them to prop up her own theories of Pagan survivals. The writings of Summers and (particularly) Murray have gone a long way toward imprinting Isobel's brand of diabolism onto the perception of modern witchcraft, even among Witches.

So that's the classic definition of a witch, established by the church and set in cement during hundreds of years of persecution and faulty folklore.

You see why I don't believe in witches?

Witch Trials in the United States

Salem immediately comes to mind, right? But our little town was kind of a late bloomer in the persecution biz. The real front runner was Connecticut, which has the dubious honor of hanging the first New England witch, forty-five years before the Salem hysteria.

And who was she? For a long time, all we really knew about her was a line in Governor Winthrop's journal: "One _____ of Windsor, arraigned and executed in Hartford for a witch." Nothing. Just a blank space. She wasn't even dignified with a name. Then, two centuries later, historians studying Town Clerk Matthew Grant's diary finally found her name, scrawled in a line of three-hundred-year-old ink: "May 26, [16]47. Alse Young was hanged."

With the discovery of that single note, Alse Young became the first person executed in New England for witchcraft.

Unlike the Salem trials, which uniformly ended in tragedy, the Connecticut trials had a few happy endings. Sarah Spencer of Colchester accused her own accusers, a Mr. and Mrs. Ackley, saying that they must have been insane to bring such a charge against her. She sued them for five hundred pounds and threw in an insanity charge to boot. Sarah didn't get her five hundred pounds, but she won her case. The court stated that it didn't believe the Ackleys were insane, but it didn't believe Sarah was a witch, either.

The Goody Clauson case began when a seventeen-year-old servant girl, Katherine Branch, fell into fits, possibly some kind of epilepsy. Sufferers of epilepsy at that time were thought to have brought the ailment onto themselves, through demon possession or curses or just plain un-Christian behavior. Katherine, probably afraid of losing her job after a seizure, started telling tales of having seen a demonic cat that tempted her with "fine things." A couple of weeks later, she began crying "witch" and accused five local women. The only one unimpressed by all this was Katherine's employer, Abigail Westcot. She said that Katherine was such a lying girl that nobody could believe one word she said, and that she personally didn't believe that any of the accused women were witches.

Appropriately enough, one of the accused women was Elizabeth Clauson. The Westcot and Clauson families had past bad blood between them, and it became obvious that Katherine accused Goody Clauson because she thought that the Westcots would be more likely to believe her witchcraft story if she accused someone whom her mistress disliked.

Here the story becomes eerily parallel to the later story of Rebecca Nurse in Salem. When Rebecca Nurse was accused of witchcraft, it turned the tide of the witchhunt. The first few accused people were on the fringes of society: Tituba the slave, and Sarah

Good and her four-year-old child, who were beggars and considered a blight on the community. Rebecca was a different sort, and if she could be accused, then no one was safe. She was a respected church member, which counted for everything in Puritan society, and had a reputation for piety and saintliness. She and her husband had raised a large family and owned a good-sized farm. Rebecca was seventy-one when she was accused and tried, and had to be carried out of her house because she was an invalid. Thirty-nine of her horrified neighbors signed petitions affirming her good name and repudiating the charge of witchcraft. Seventy-six of Goody Clauson's neighbors signed a document attesting to her good character. Since it was thought that only a witch would come to the aid of another witch, this was outstandingly courageous. Unfortunately, the tactic didn't work in Rebecca Nurse's case.

But it did in Elizabeth Clauson's. The court dismissed the charges against three of the accused as too flimsy. At first, the court was deadlocked on Clauson, but finally she was found not guilty. Another accused witch, Mercy Disborough, was found guilty.

Mercy's case was reconsidered after several neighbors stuck up for her good name. The Connecticut court seemed to have better sense than the court in Salem, because it threw out "spectral evidence," a key factor—and sometimes the *only* factor—in the Salem accusations. The Connecticut court also said that it didn't believe "swimming" a witch was evidence of guilt, and that "witch marks" shouldn't be allowed as evidence unless validated by a physician. Most important, it stated that the accuser Katherine's evidence carried a "suspicion of her counterfeiting." In other words, the court knew a faker when it saw one. Too bad the Salem judges weren't as astute.

It's interesting that recent theories about the Salem trials have tried to excuse away the dismal behavior of the teenage accusers as having been brought about by ergot poisoning due to tainted wheat in bread. What this theory doesn't take into account are the facts that:

1. The accusing "afflicted" girls were able to throw their fits on cue.
2. The fits seemed to come and go on a regular basis for a period of about nine months (anybody poisoned for that long on a day-to-day basis would have been in a bad way, but the girls were otherwise healthy—that is, when they weren't screaming and whirling around like Britney Spears on caffeine overload).
3. None of the judges, or the accused, or the onlookers seem to have been poisoned.
4. Some of the girls, when asked why they accused certain people, replied, "For sport. We must have some sport."
5. When the governor finally pulled the plug on the witch trials, the fits came to an abrupt end. We're supposed to believe that the poisoned bread just suddenly went away after people had been eating it all that time? And that this tainted wheat never grew in Salem again, since there were no more recorded outbreaks of anyone having similar fits?

So the theory that the poor little darlings weren't responsible for their heinous actions doesn't quite hold up. I'm only surprised that no one's advanced the theory that they all had attention deficit disorder.

The Fallacy of the Burning Times

So what's the point of all this? It's this: The way Wicca and Witchcraft is presented today owes quite a bit to the ideas that came out of the witch trials and early persecutions of heretics.

And many of the misconceptions are perpetrated by Witches and Wiccans.

The black robes, the idea of brooms and "flying ointment" as part of our history, the emphasis on magic, the idea that Witches are formed into covens and meet at night, the so-called secret books of lore and rituals, and much more of the trappings of modern Witchcraft all stem from the ideas first presented by the witch hunters or those searching out heresy. We profess to revile the witch hunts at the same time that we've adopted some of the ideas and symbols that didn't exist before them.

We insist that these ideas were part of the ancient practice of witchcraft, because we don't take the time—or have the inclination—to read real history and anthropology to find out where these ideas originated and how accurate they were. We accept the word of some Wiccan historians who may have applied their own particular bias to historical fact in an effort to establish Wicca or Witchcraft without question as a Pagan survival, specifically of a Goddess-centered matriarchal culture in which everything was peaceful and productive until the rise of men and Christianity.

This is the fallacy of the Burning Times: that the persecution of witches or heretics had anything to do with crushing a Pagan religious survival, or that modern Wiccans have a right to claim those times as our "holocaust." Since Wiccans insist that our religion has nothing to do with diabolism, or with the Christian idea of a witch, how can we now insist that the victims of the witch hysteria had anything to do with us? How can we insist on invoking the "victims" as symbols of injustice when those victims were clearly not connected with our history? If there is any injustice, it is in our shameless exploitation of these tragic people.

The idea that Wicca, especially, is a survival of Pagan religion doesn't take into consideration the time periods. If the aim of the church of Rome was to exterminate Paganism, why did it take them so long to start doing it? Waiting until 1245 meant a pretty slow start, since Paganism was supposed to have been around and intact for centuries before that. In actuality, most Pagans were long gone by then, and their tribal religions with them.

Those Wiccans who insist on the existence of a Book of Shadows or a Grimoire supposedly written by medieval peasant witches during the Burning Times and passed down intact for generations have no idea of either the literacy factor, the availability of paper, ink, or bookbinding, or the correct period of history during which the witch hysteria took place.

Those who say that the witch hysteria was an attempt by the emerging male medical schools to wipe out heathen herbalists or "wise women" overlook the fact that there were no doctors or medical schools in most places, and that healing with herbs was something that everyone knew how to do, out of necessity. Even in the days of the ancient Greeks, there were schools of medicine established, and Greek doctors were prized in the Roman culture, but none of these medical men was persecuting any witches in order to establish a medical hierarchy.

Unfortunately, many Wiccans read nothing except that which supports the theory of unbroken Pagan and Witch survivals. They get impatient with anything that counters it, often saying that "history was written by the winners." History may have been, but real, respectable, and impersonal anthropological research was not and is not.

There are two types of faulty logic that come into play here. One is *confirmation bias*, in which you notice and accept only those facts that confirm your beliefs, while ignoring or undervaluing facts that contradict them. Another is *communal reinforcement*, which happens when a theory or a claim is repeated throughout a community so often that the community accepts it as true, whether it is or not. Some Wiccan writers and teachers have been passing on misinformation or selective scholarship for so long that it's become part of our mythology, passed on from one presumably authoritative source to another. Many Wiccans don't read anything except Wiccan books, many of which simply repeat the real or erroneous information found in other Wiccan books.

It's as if we're afraid that if one sacred claim about Wicca is wrong, then the whole shebang will collapse. This is nonsense. There are holes in Christianity and Judaism and Hinduism that you could drive a truck through, and the religions are doing just fine. In fact, many religious scholars concern themselves with exactly those holes and inconsistencies. The Bible has sure been through enough rewrites.

If you're serious about Wicca, reading source material outside the Wiccan framework should be part of the work you need to do. Don't just read *Aradia* or *The Witch-Cult in Western Europe* or some of the works that insist that Wicca is derived from pre-Christian matriarchal cultures. Maybe it is and maybe it isn't. Read the conflicting research and make your own decision. *Aradia* in particular is considered to be either a fake perpetrated on its author, Charles Leland, or something he made up himself to prop up his own theories. But how would you know that if you've only read *Aradia*? And do you think that it makes a heck of a lot of difference to the Strega who follow it? Maybe you'll read the arguments against its authenticity, but decide that *they're* the bogus claims. The point is that you need to read enough to make intelligent choices, not just follow whatever you're told. You don't have to agree with every single point of a religion to be able to find comfort in it.

We're appalled by what Gerald Gardner called the Burning Times, and yet we do everything we can to perpetuate its picture of witches. We rail against "stereotypes" while reinforcing them. We're afraid to examine our own religion too closely, in case the facts don't match what we want to believe, as if that would invalidate the religion. And then we bemoan the fact that Wicca isn't taken seriously.

Maybe it's time to start asking ourselves what we can do to change that.

3

Deities

IF YOU READ ONLY ONE CHAPTER, READ THIS ONE

Experienced Wiccans are always hearing the same questions from seekers: "I think I might be a Witch or a Pagan. How can I know for sure?" And we're usually stuck for an answer, because there doesn't seem to be one until we know what the seeker is really asking. Is the seeker considering Witchcraft or Wicca because she suspects she might have psychic abilities? Is he considering Wicca because no other religion gives him the spiritual fulfillment he needs? Is she attracted to the religion for reasons she can't put into words?

The advice we would give seekers in each category is complex. But the *answer* is fairly simple, provided we first ask one question of our own: *What is your personal belief about deities?*

In almost all cases, you know you're a Wiccan or Pagan because you believe in the gods and feel a connection with one or all of them. If you just want to work magic and leave religion out of it, you're definitely not suited for Wicca or Paganism. Maybe some forms of ceremonial magic or folk magic with no involvement with gods would work for you, and there *are* atheist Witches who work magic with no religious overtones.

But without deities, there is no religion. There's no reason for it otherwise. As we saw earlier, religion is the set of beliefs and rules that we make for ourselves in order to strengthen our connection with the gods. Religion is the way we communicate with them, honor them, and thank them. Religion is highly personal—which is why we can make up our own rituals, and they're just as true as any other. Religion is also there to help us through our lives, to give us moral or ethical guidelines, or just to satisfy our longing for ceremony at times of emotional need, like weddings or funerals. You can have your religion as simple or as complicated as you want, but the one thing it must do is connect you and the gods.

This is why it makes no difference whether Wicca is based on ancient Pagan practices or if it was completely made up in the 1950s. And it makes no difference if the only believer in your religion is you, or if it has millions of believers and billions of bucks. If it's real to *somebody,* it's a real religion. And I'm not getting into judgment calls on somebody's belief system being bad or good as a criterion for determining whether a religion is real or false: That may be a test of the ethical code of a religion, but it isn't a test of the *validity* of that religion. Most people were appalled by David Koresh's cult in Waco or the Heaven's Gate people who killed themselves with poisoned pudding or those sects that let their kids die because they didn't believe in medical treatment. Being misguided, or running counter to popular opinion, or even breaking the law doesn't mean that these people weren't practicing a real religion. You have to wonder about the leadership and the followers of sects like that, but you can't deny that they were religious. If your religious practices are against the law and you go to jail, it's still religion. But making judgments on the correctness of someone else's religion is what leads to holy wars and religious genocide.

Plenty of people are appalled by Wicca, too. Doesn't mean we're not a religion. Even if we lost our protection under the First Amendment and no longer qualified for tax-exempt status (more about this in a later chapter), as long as we have just one believer, we're still a religion.

Religion and a relationship with the gods can relieve the sometimes terrible isolation of life. The writer George Sand not only made up her own religion, but she also made up her own god, a deity she called "Corambe." She said she never knew where the name came from. This deity was a constant help and reassurance to her through her rather tempestuous childhood.

Are the gods real? How do we know? We don't. Gods are, in some ways, invented by humans. That is to say, those energies and spirits are real, but we have transformed them into anthropomorphic forms and ideas that are easier for us to identify with. It's simpler and more personal to understand the energies that inspire us to love if we call those energies Aphrodite. In our stories about them, we have invested the gods with emotions, passions, and character flaws like our own, but have acknowledged that they possess the divine powers to overcome those flaws. By our association with them, we also acknowledge the divine spark in ourselves, gained by our connection with the gods through religion, to help us overcome the same failings.

In worshiping the gods, we have given them power as they have given it to us. It's a reciprocal agreement, a shared energy that grows as it is used. We have strengthened the power and personalities of our gods as they have shared their inherent power with us.

As an example, the explorer and adventurer Alexandra David-Neel, who traveled extensively in Tibet, learned how to create a thought-form. This is done by concentrating the power of the mind so that it interacts with external or divine powers to create a tangible entity, sometimes in human form. David-Neel's thought-form, called a *tulpa,* was a jolly little man so real that others could interact with it. In fact, she had some trouble finally getting rid of it.

But the mental power of David-Neel and the reciprocal power of the energies out there in the universe combined to create something that was part of both of them. That's why I say that when we work with the gods, they strengthen the qualities in us that they represent, and we strengthen their presence in the universe.

Maybe it's sentimental—okay, I *know* it's sentimental—but I like to think of the ancient Pagan gods as having fallen asleep as their worship declined. Now that their worship has revived, so have they. Old Jehovah, originally a vengeance demon and one who demanded he be worshiped as the only God, must be plenty pissed off now that he's sharing the divine stage with Jupiter, Osiris, and Odin again. And considering his followers' low opinion of women, he must be frothing at the mouth now that Diana, Isis, and Macha are back.

Are these energies actually energies within ourselves? Are they simply emotions, ideas, brain chemistry, elements of the mind and intelligence, with nothing to do with universal energies *outside* ourselves? Maybe. But if you believe that we were created by those outside energies, that they somehow came together to begin all life, then you can believe that we, as part of that process, are part of the gods. That's why I believe in the divine creation of human life *and* I believe in Darwin's theories. Something had to start the evolutionary process, and I choose to believe that the original spark of life was divine in nature.

What I just can't wrap my mind around is Adam, Eve, Cain, and Abel, the first dysfunctional family. Somebody's yankin' our chains with that one.

Were the gods ever real, living people? We know that some of them were. For example, the Romans deified their emperors on a regular basis. The Emperor Vespasian, who had a wry sense of humor, said on his deathbed, "Oh dear; I feel myself turning into a god!"* Deifying the emperors was really more of a personification of the qualities of that emperor as he related to the Roman Empire as a whole, kind of like Uncle Sam being the personification of America. And while we don't pray to Uncle Sam, except at

*Not all emperors made it to divine status. Nero, for one, was never deified.

tax time, the Romans did pray to the deified emperors. This also helped the conquered provinces feel connected to Rome, although I'm not sure how appreciative a conquered Briton actually was as he contemplated a statue of Vespasian, whose legions had crushed his homeland.

Ancestor worship was also popular.* Since the spirits of your dead relatives were now in the underworld, they were in a better position to intercede for you with the gods. The Roman underworld was not necessarily a place of torment or punishment; everybody went there, bad or good. You were judged and assigned to the Elysian Fields if you were a warrior who had fallen in battle, or someone who had served Rome well; to the Plain of Asphodel, where you just carried on with daily activities; or, if you'd offended the gods, to Tartarus, where the Furies invented imaginative tortures especially for you. Also, the Romans believed that spirits could come back and terrorize you if you failed to honor them. Any sensible Roman had an altar to his household gods, including his ancestors, in his home. Relatives were honored as spirits, but not as gods: The emperors were deified because most of them had been very important priests in the state religion— okay, *and* for political reasons.

The Christian Church owes quite a lot to this practice. It also adopted the Pagan custom of deifying dead people, although Christians call it canonization. The church will tell you that saints aren't gods, because there's only one true God (yeah, yeah, *that* old song and dance), but if it looks like a duck and quacks like a duck . . .

The church also turned Pagan gods into saints. It was much easier to convert Pagans if Christians took the attributes of the gods and gave them new personifications more in line with the Christian philosophy. The most famous example of this is the conversion of several chthonic mother goddesses into Mary, Jesus' mom.

---

*And still is, if you ask the Daughters of the American Revolution and the *Mayflower* descendants.

I find it a more than a little ironic that the African slaves, brought to this country against their will and forbidden to honor their tribal gods, simply turned the Catholic saints into gods again by worshiping their old gods under the names of saints. That's one reason why Caribbean-derived Voudoun has such heavy Catholic overtones, and why many Voudouns are purging them from the religion, making their way back to the Yoruba roots.

The True Nature of Mysteries

Many people coming into Wicca have heard about "Mysteries," and they assume that after training, these Mysteries will be magically opened to them, or explained to them. And Wiccans themselves are guilty of referring to coven or Trad secrets as "our Mysteries," when what they're referring to are actually rules, rituals, practices, or imparted wisdom that the coven protects (or so they like to think) with oaths. When you hear of information being "oathbound," this is what is meant by the phrase: You take an oath not to reveal what you learn from that coven or group.

Wicca picked up this phrase about Mysteries from classical Pagan religions called Mystery Religions or Mystery Cults, or simply Mysteries, the best known being the Mysteries of Eleusis and the Orphic Mysteries. They were Mysteries not so much because what went on during the religious rites was not written down and was not talked about outside the confines of the religious worship, but because the individual religious experience could not be explained, since it was different for each worshiper and varied in its intensity and in the resultant changes in the person. Have you ever listened to someone describe his or her dreams? No matter how intense an experience it was for the dreamer, and no matter that the dream may have changed his or her life, it's only marginally interesting to you. It may make a good story—and a lot of novels have been born in just this way—but it isn't going to affect you as it affected the dreamer.

Likewise, the real "Mysteries" in Wicca cannot be taught, or even communicated. They must be experienced, and they're different for everyone. You'll hear me say this a lot in this book, and that's because it's the one thing I really want you to understand. This highly personal, individual experience is why taking some oath to "protect" a Mystery is laughable: You could chatter on about a Mystery for hours, and it wouldn't mean a thing to anyone else. You could duplicate the exact ritual of any coven or Trad and still not experience any spiritual change; then you could be sitting alone and meditating and a life-changing revelation suddenly comes to you.

The ongoing process of spiritual evolution takes place in stages. This is why "initiations" and "elevations" and the other ceremonial folderol of Wicca are, at bottom, simply window dressing, something like diplomas given out at graduation to prove you've learned the rules and regulations. They may mean that you've learned more about the Trad's practices, but they don't necessarily mean you're closer to the gods. They're not *from* the gods: Believe me, when you've had an initiation from the gods, you'll know it. People say they feel something at their coven initiations or when they're conferred degrees, but much of that is simply conditioned behavior. Like most life passages, we feel what we think we're supposed to feel: We're reacting to a stimulus, the stimulus being the mystical trappings surrounding ceremony and our resultant emotional response. It's the reason that people cry at weddings and graduations.

But the true initiation, the true growth and change, is something that we can neither control nor explain. It is a personal epiphany, a moment of realization that happens in an instant, although it could take years of work and study and just plain living to produce it. You can't mistake it when it happens, and you can't go back to where you were before it hit you. And lest you think that this spiritual initiation is all happy-happy white light and good times, it isn't. It's sometimes a pain so profound that we are forced to change.

These epiphanies, or true initiations, the real Mysteries, can happen any number of times in our lives, and at any time.

When these things happen, they come from the gods. No matter how many books you read, or don't read, or how many degrees and initiations you've collected, and how many Trads or covens you've been in, it all means nothing. Only the touch of the gods is real and life changing. Only the light of the gods is the true illumination of the soul.

Gods and Religious Systems

As I've said, religion is the system we've devised to honor the gods. That's not to say that the gods haven't had a hand in devising those systems. As we've also seen, much information can come to us from the gods themselves. Our religious systems sometimes came about by trial and error: You sacrificed a ram to Jupiter in a supplication for his help on a particular matter, and, sure enough, you received his divine aid. Therefore, you concluded that sacrificing a ram was what Jupiter wanted you to do for him. He could also communicate with you through these animals: The entrails were examined as divinatory signs. You burned frankincense to honor Mercurius, and he helped you because he knew you'd taken the trouble to honor him with what he liked.

The idea of burnt offerings—the blood and entrails of animals and the smoke of resinous incense or of particular woods—came from the belief that the gods, not needing actual food, thrived instead on the smoke of particular substances rising from the altar fires. These were called "fumigations."

Through ages of religious practices, humans came to determine what the gods required. And to honor those gods and receive their help, you need to follow the particular invocations and rituals belonging to those individual gods, or pantheon of gods.

You'll have to decide this on your own, but it's my theory that the gods you honor and work with every day will determine how you practice Wicca or Paganism. For instance, if you observe the usual eight Sabbats, those are of Celtic origin. Lughnasad may be just peachy for the Celtic Lugh, but Jupiter, Osiris, Isis, or Athene aren't likely to respond to celebration of that Sabbat. It just isn't the kind of ritual they're familiar with or one they expect.

If you care enough about a god to work with him or her, and he or she has been good enough to bless you, you can make the effort to learn about the god's worship, including his or her festival days, the kinds and forms of prayer acceptable to that deity, and the incense or fumigation (if any) that he or she prefers. Although we can't be 100 percent accurate about the forms of ancient worship, with a little study we can devise pretty good approximations.

If you're going to practice Wicca, keep away from the gods of Santeria, Voudoun, Mayo Palombre, and Candomble. Not because they're dangerous, but because they have their own religions with their own rules. You can't just plop those gods down in the middle of a Wiccan Circle—they expect certain rituals and preparations to have been made, and that their followers have the proper knowledge to interact with them. These gods are not really compatible with Wicca, and most Wiccans have no idea how to show them the proper respect. Also, many of these religions consider "Witches" to be totally incompatible with their beliefs. And despite their claim to "magickal channeling," most Wiccans have no preparation for the phenomenon of religious possession.* These powerful spirits are very old and very precise in what they want and need, and Wicca in no way prepares you to handle it, especially if the spirit needs an animal sacrifice, which is not unusual. If you feel drawn to these gods, then drop Wicca and find a priest or priestess of the religion of those gods to instruct you. Like Isaac Bonewits says: Possession is nine-tenths of the *loa*.

Asatru, the ancient Norse religion, is not Wicca, and you would be well advised to learn this now rather than later. If you insist on

---

Most is the key word here. See chapter 6, on Traditions, for Wiccans who practice trance possession.

the Wiccan Rede, you're going to run into a conflict with Asatru, which includes powerful warrior gods who do not like to be forced into the Wiccan mold.

More foolish is the inexperienced or unprepared Wiccan who decides to invoke the destroyer gods because he or she believes that working with those gods creates the impression that he or she is a powerful magician, working with dangerous powers. Working with Kali or Lilith is just not advised unless you're ready for a total life change.

What are the effects of invoking powers like this? A couple of examples:

Kali, the Hindu goddess of destruction, is one of the most loved goddesses in that pantheon, although she's terrifying. There's a reason that she looks the way she does in most of her statuary: black-faced, wild-eyed, dancing on the body of the half-dead Krishna and almost destroying him in the process, oblivious to his pain. It is this very terror that her worshipers invoke: Once called, Kali will take over your life, bringing dramatic and sometimes agonizing changes that make you face your worst fears. Once you work through those fears—if you remain sane—Kali works in her aspect of comforter to help you rebuild your life, this time freed of the fears that you had to face and conquer. If you didn't conquer them, that's no concern of hers: You called, she answered. She will not change into a benevolent goddess until you've proved yourself worthy of her help.

Lilith is a Sumerian goddess whom the Hebrews transformed into a demon. In the Hebrew stories of the creation of humans, Lilith was Adam's original mate, who was cast out because she refused to take a subordinate position to him. And why *should* a goddess take a subordinate position to a man? The reason that many feminists invoke Lilith is that they need to cast off the timidity and rectitude that have been conditioned in modern women, in order to fight the battles for female equality. This was especially important to hard-line feminists of the 1960s and 1970s, who were likely to go to jail or worse while fighting for privileges and equalities that today's women take for granted. (Although there's still a long way to go in that regard.) Lilith would give you the strength you needed, but you had to be unafraid of it, and of the consequences: If you were concerned with keeping your image as one of the popular girls or a sexpot or a good wife and selfless mother, you just didn't invoke her. That was baggage that women warriors in a battle situation just didn't need. Women who want to work with Lilith have to keep one thing in mind: Lilith destroyed her children in order to fight her battles. And while this is pretty damn extreme, and many feminists certainly would reject this idea, women who are not engaged in dedicating their lives to fighting for equality or any other extreme cause would be advised *not* to invoke this goddess. Invoking Lilith doesn't mean you kill your own kids. It just means that children are secondary to the greater goals. Feminists who are also mothers would be insane to invoke her—better to go with a less extreme goddess, so there's no conflict between the needs of your kids and the time you devote to your cause. Lilith's struggle is for the betterment of future generations of all children, not just your own.

Powerful transformative gods should never be invoked lightly, without a thorough research on the history and rituals particular to those gods. Actually, *no* god should ever be invoked lightly.

The Myth of "the Goddess" and "the God"

The rise of new-wave feminism and the rise of Wicca came at about the same time, especially in America, so it's no surprise that female scholars and writers were determined to link Wicca with research on ancient goddess-worshiping cultures, and to establish the European witch hysteria as a "women's holocaust." Working from the theories of Margaret Murray, historians Merlin Stone, Matilda Joslyn Gage,* Marija Gimbutas, and others advanced the

*Gage originally devised the "nine million" figure to represent the victims of the European witch hysteria.

feminist cause by slanting historical and archaeological evidence toward the veneration of a universal Earth Mother goddess worshiped throughout ancient European cultures. A matriarchy or woman-dominated culture was supposed to have been devoid of the features of male-dominated cultures: war, greed, and crime.

As Ronald Hutton pointed out, ". . . the American feminist spirituality movement generally wanted a Goddess, partly as a convenient abstraction for female spiritual power, and partly as a straightforward answer to dominant male monotheism."*

Unfortunately, the existence of a universal single goddess and a woman-dominated, peaceful culture can't be proved. The trend of recent scholarship is to discredit, or at least to reexamine, the conclusions of these feminist scholars. Some Wiccans are outraged by this, sometimes to the point of irrationality.

One case *for* a single-goddess theory in Wicca comes from an early work of literature, Apuleius's *The Golden Ass,* which is examined more closely in chapter 12. In this work, Apuleius speaks of a great goddess, Isis, who appears to him and tells him that she is worshiped under many names in many cultures, but is one goddess. This story provided the basis for one of Wicca's most entrenched rituals, the Charge of the Goddess, written (for all practical purposes) by Doreen Valiente, when she revised Gerald Gardner's rituals. Apuleius's story is, alas, a work of fiction.

The problem with the widespread acceptance of these "one universal Goddess" theories, at least for pantheist Pagans and Wiccans, is that it encourages a homogenized, white-bread, and featureless "goddess" in which is blended all the attributes of the hundreds or thousands of Pagan goddesses. The same has been done to gods, who are now simply referred to as "the God," the consort of "the Goddess." What we have lost, or are rapidly in the process of losing, is the wonderfully complex system of deities from all cultures and all tribes, each of whom has a personality of

*Ronald Hutton, *The Triumph of the Moon,* Oxford University Press, New York, 1999.

his or her own, and a rich store of legends about the adventures of the gods. This makes Wicca and Paganism fit neatly into the fast 'n' easy American culture: no more detailed studying of ancient history and mythologies! All the gods and goddesses are really only aspects of the one universal energy! It doesn't help that these two homogeneous gods have been packaged and marketed to the masses, and have become more sterile and squeaky clean than Barbie and Ken, purged of all that nasty "negative energy."

It's almost enough to make Kali weep.

If you're going to refer to "the Goddess" and "the God," at least make a study of the various deities, preferably in various pantheons, so you'll have a more complete idea of who comes under those two general headings.

"Adopt a Deity"

In his terrific little book *50 Things You Can Do to Advance Pagan Religion*, modern pantheist Cassius Julianus proposes that you "adopt a deity." Everyone knows about the major gods, but in every culture there were lesser-known gods who held important places in religion. Also, there were tribal gods and gods of lesser-known religions whose practice has died out. Cassius recommends that you "Find a minor deity that you have never heard of before, and research the deity's history and function. Work with them. Get to know their powers and purpose. You may be the only living priest or priestess of that deity, but at least they are active in this world again. We must not let any part of our divine heritage be forgotten."

The Big Four:
Greek, Roman, Celtic, and Egyptian Gods

The nature of gods is complex and fascinating to study, and researching the old stories and rituals is something you're going to want to do on your own if you're serious about religion. For example, you'll find that it isn't completely accurate to refer to Apollo as simply the Sun god. Like most of the gods, he evolved through many ages and cultures, each culture adding various attributes until Apollo's duties took on complex meanings and intricate symbolism, some of them very dark and solemn.

I'm giving you some short descriptions of the major deities in the pantheons most often invoked by Wiccans, but this is only a starting point. You'll want to carry on the study of the gods for yourself.

I haven't included the Norse gods, the Aesir, because Asatru isn't part of Wicca, but you might want to study them because there are some *great* stories and fabulous heroes in Norse sagas. The most interesting of these is the Nibelungenlied, a sensational story of the hero Siegfried (not the tiger guy Roy's friend; this is another Siegfried), a dragon, a sexy warrior queen, a dwarf warlord, trolls, twelve giants, and a cave full of treasure. It's got everything. Why Spielberg hasn't filmed it is beyond me, but it did produce a series of Wagner operas so long that to hear them all takes four days. You'll want to bring a few snacks and a six-pack.

The Gods of Greece and Rome

There's such a crossover between the Greek and Roman gods because the centuries of incessant wars, reconciliation, alliances, and trade between the two cultures made an exchange of gods almost inevitable. Rome never had a problem with imported gods: "The more the merrier" was their attitude, resulting in a list of festivals and holidays that outnumbered the actual days in the year. The Romans were originally not all that cultured; *civilized*, but not cultured. Nobody could top them in the operations of government, war, finances, and bureaucracy. For the graceful arts of poetry, sculpture, decoration, rhetoric, storytelling, and even medicine, though, the Romans looked to the Greeks. Consequently, a lot of Greek culture—and the Greek gods who went with it—found its way to Rome.

Zeus (Roman Jupiter, Jove), the king and father of the gods, in both pantheons. Zeus's name is derived from Sanskrit for "bright sky," which identifies him with the sky and all its phenomena: rain, lightning, thunder, gathering clouds, storms. He presides over all things and all gods, the entire course of nature. In Rhodes and Crete, worshipers celebrated him also as a god of death and rebirth: The winter death of nature was supposed to be the death of the god. In Rome, he was honored as Jupiter Optimus Maximus, Jupiter Best and Greatest, the protector of Roman power; Jupiter Stator, the bringer of victory; and Jupiter Freretrius, to whom spoils of war were offered. His name is a combination of *Jovis* and *pater*, father. He is also Lucetius, the bringer of light of the sun at day and the full moon at night. The eagle and the oak are sacred to him, which is why the symbol of Rome is the eagle. Jupiter, however, had a few problems with his magnificent temple on the Capitoline Hill: It kept burning down, in B.C.E. 83, B.C.E. 78, C.E. 80, and C.E. 82. Various emperors were always trying to come up with the cash to rebuild it.

Hera (Roman Juno), the mother and queen of the gods, wife and sister to Zeus and Jupiter. In Rome, she is Juno Lucina, bringer of light and goddess of childbirth and marriage. She is also Juno Moneta, the admonisher, who gave good advice. This is the root of the word *money*, because Roman coins were minted at her temple (her hubby may have the power, but she's got the gold).

Poseidon (Roman Neptune), The god of the sea. At first, it seems strange that both sea gods are also equestrian gods, horses being so close to the earth. But the sea foam on the great waves was supposed to be the horses of Poseidon, so that's how the association came about. Poseidon has two very different aspects: As god of the stormy seas, a bull is offered to him as a sacrifice, since the bull was a symbol of the storm. As god of calm waters, his symbol is the dolphin. This is a changeable god: He sends tempests, but he also sends favorable winds. He gives victory in sea battles, and protects fishermen. The blows from his trident were thought to cause earthquakes beneath the sea.

Phoebus Apollo (same in Rome), is the god of light, not just the sun god. Actually, to the Greeks, the sun god was Helios, who drove his flaming chariot across the morning sky; later on, Helios and Apollo were thought of as the same god. He is the god of pure, life-giving light that defies the darkness, an association of complex meanings. His oracles were definitely not all light and sweetness. Consulting his priestess at Delphi, the sibyl, was a fairly terrifying procedure: You wound your way down a steep, dark path in a cave until you came upon a pitch-black underground room lit by a shaft of light, where you consulted Apollo's half-mad prophetic priestess and tried to make sense of what she told you as the god spoke through her. Apollo is also the god of music, healing, and male beauty.

Hermes (Roman Mercury or Mercurius), the messenger of the gods, also the god of rhetoric, commerce and prosperity . . . and incidentally patron of tricksters and thieves. His son, Autolycus, was the most accomplished of these. He is also the god of sports (invoked *plenty* around here when the Sox are playing), and it was Hermes who taught Apollo to play the lyre. His symbol is the caduceus, that staff with the entwined snakes that you'll see in doctor's offices and at pharmacies—not surprising, since he's also god of medicine. And if your doctor didn't turn out to be the greatest, Hermes also guides the shades of the dead to the underworld.

Ares (Roman Mars). Interestingly enough, Mars began as an agricultural god, invoked to protect the fields and herds. As Rome expanded—which made battle necessary—he became the god of war. When hostilities broke out, his priests struck his symbolic shield with his lance and cried, "Mars, *vigila!*" (Mars, awake!) As a battle god, Mars is rather civilized, since the Roman legions had war down to an exact science. On the other hand, the Greek Ares is wild and bloodthirsty, rampaging around in his chariot with his equally wild sister, Eris, goddess of discord and strife. A pair not to be messed with. Oddly enough, Ares is the father of Eros, the god of love, born of a rather torrid affair he had with Aphrodite, who was married to . . .

Hephaestus (Roman Vulcan or Volcanus). Nobody could understand what Aphrodite, the goddess of love, ever saw in Hephaestus, the lame and ugly god of fire and the forge. She was also goddess of beauty, however, and recognized a true artist when she saw one. Hephaestus presides over the arts produced by fire, such as metalworking and glassblowing. Both are gods of volcanoes, but Vulcan has the stronger association.

Demeter (Roman Ceres). One of the most overarching stories in Wicca is the tale of the Earth/Corn Mother, Demeter, bringing winter and starvation to the world as she searches for her daughter, Persephone, who has been kidnapped by Hades and made queen of the underworld. When Persephone is reunited with her mom, spring returns to the earth. Hades and Demeter agree to alternate custody, and the world gets alternating seasons, death and rebirth. If you're going to be Wiccan, you need to research this story, and the two goddesses Demeter and Persephone in more depth. Even covens that profess to be staunchly Celtic celebrate it in one form or another.

Artemis (Roman Diana). The virgin moon goddesses Diana and Artemis are so important in Wicca that you need to become very familiar with them, too. They're quite complex, identified with Hecate, goddess of Witchcraft and hidden mysteries, and with other moon and night goddesses such as Selene, Bendis, and Britomartis. Diana and Artemis are goddesses of the hunt, symbolized by the bow and quiver, and the stag. Diana's sacred grove at Lake Nemi was the home of the Rex Nemorensis, the priest of Diana who had to kill his predecessor in combat. Virbius, god of the forest and the chase, was worshiped at Nemi with Diana.

Athene (Roman Minerva) was originally a goddess of war, and is still regarded as a protector and defender, which is why she appears in armor. But, Athena is also an agricultural goddess who gave humans the olive tree and taught them how to plow. Because of her good advice and counsel, she is goddess of wisdom and learning, wit and intellect, art and science, and patroness of teachers, spinners, weavers, artisans, poets, writers, and painters. She also invented the flute and trumpet, and presides over music and dancing.

Aphrodite (Roman Venus). To the Romans, the goddess of love was originally goddess of spring (duties later assumed by Maia), and flowers and vines (Flora, the Bona Dea, took over this area). She is also Venus Genetrix, mother of the Roman people. Aphrodite is another old and complex deity: She also presides over shifting winds, seas and skies, storms and lightning, and is sometimes portrayed as armed (which partially explains her association with Ares).

Hestia (Roman Vesta). These days, people make jokes about Vestal Virgins, but if you lived in ancient Rome, that would have been a really bad move. The six priestesses of Vesta, goddess of hearth and home, tended the sacred flame in Vesta's temple, regarded as the hearth of the state. If this fire ever went out, things looked bleak for Rome, because its fortunes were linked to the flame, and to the sanctity of the Vestals. The official end of the Roman Empire came in C.E. 382, when Rome was no longer the center of the world, and the flame was extinguished.

Pan (Roman Silvanus and Faunus), the god of hills, woods, flocks, herdsmen, and hunters, who plays sweet music on his own invention, the panpipes. He is very much a god of nature, including the amorous nature of humans. He's bearded, with two horns, shaggy hair, and goat's feet—which, considering the number of nymphs he's supposed to have chased, certainly didn't slow him down. *Panic* originally meant the sudden terror caused by the solitude of a forest. Pan was supposed to have inspired such fright in the Persians that they fled the Greek city of Marathon.

Hades/Pluto (Roman Dis or Dis Pater) is god of the underworld, and rules there with his queen, **Persephone (Roman Proserpina).** His region consists of three regions and five rivers, including the Styx, which the dead must cross to reach the underworld. He is the only god with no name, only the name of his realm, which refers to the hidden wealth of the earth. Hades is not the god of death (that's **Mors,** a beautiful youth). The Romans gave Dis Pater (Father Dis) his own altar and temple, and sacrificed to him, but the Greeks thought that Hades was inexorable and unmoved by sacrifice and prayer.

The Gods of Rome

Some gods were strictly Roman, mainly the very ancient gods who were vital to Rome when it was still an agricultural society, moving toward urbanization.

Janus is represented with two faces as the god of portals, beginnings and endings. He presides over the beginning of everything in Rome, and his festival is January 1. On New Year's Day, Romans celebrated his festival by exchanging presents. There was a covered passage in the city dedicated to Janus, which was opened during war and closed during peace; we can assume that during the expansion of the empire, this passage was pretty much a 24/7 operation.

Saturn introduced agriculture, civilization, and government to the Romans. This is most likely another case of a real person being deified, since he was thought to have been an ancient king whose reign was a golden age. The seven-day December festival of Saturnalia, with parties, presents, and the Lord of Misrule (a slave or fool turned "master" for a day) commemorates the Golden Age of Saturn.

Ops or **Dea Dia** is the goddess of plenty and prosperity, wife of Saturn.

Fortuna is the goddess of fortune and fate. Talk about a goddess with many names: Fortuna is also Fortuna Primagenia, who determines the destiny of a child at birth; Fortuna Privata, of family life; Fortuna Liberum, of children; Fortuna Mulebris, of women; Fortuna Virginalis, of virgins and young women; Fortuna Virilis, of women's happiness in marriage (think about the implications of that one as the root word of *virile*); Fortuna Bona and Mala (good and evil fortune); Blanda (flattering); Dubia (doubtful);

Brevis (fickle); Manens (constant); and many more. Obviously, Fortuna is to be honored in her many forms, and invoked for many reasons, and she had a *lot* of temples. One is still standing in Rome, the Temple of Portunus: **Portunus** and Fortuna were guardians of the Roman harbor.

Egeria, goddess of fountains and childbirth. She was supposed to be one of the Camenae, prophetic nymphs. She was the consort and counselor of King Pompilius, who used to sneak out to the sacred ground at night to meet her; on her advice he founded the religious system of Rome and laid the foundation for the social and governmental system. When Pompilius died, Egeria's grief was so profound that the goddess Diana changed her into a fountain. Some scholars think that Egeria was based on a real woman, another case of someone being deified and a fabulous legend growing up around her.

Bellona was a really busy girl at one point, since she is the Roman goddess of war. Whenever they were about to stick it to somebody, the Romans would bang a lance on a special column in front of Bellona's temple, then fling the lance as a formal declaration of war.

Lupercus and Luperca, deities of fertility, and protectors of flocks from wolves. The Lupercalia, held on February 15, was a popular festival with Roman women. Wives who wanted to get pregnant flocked around the scantily clad priests of Lupercus, who would smack them with a rawhide thong as a mark of the god's favor.

The domestic gods. The **lares** originally presided over your house, and the **penates** over your fields and roads, but in time they became the most personal of Roman gods, with the lares being associated with the family and the penates with the house and especially the larder or food storerooms. They are actually the shades of the benevolent dead. The **lar familiaris** is the founder of your family; the lares are the shades of your ancestors and should be honored at all family celebrations. Modern Roman Pagans keep a lararium, an altar with family photos, in their homes. The penates are now gods of the home; the dining table is sacred to them as a sign of prosperity, and they are honored along with the lares.

Mithras. Okay, he was actually a Persian god, but he definitely made it big in Rome. Mithras was a sun god, and a god of battle in the cause of justice. Naturally, the Roman legions were all *over* this god, and his worship was solidly entrenched, especially when the Emperor Commodus became an initiate. The worship itself is interesting: It was held in caves and was secretive and fraternal, with a system of seven degrees of initiation into the Mysteries. Sound familiar? At one level there was a degree for women, sort of like the Order of the Eastern Star for wives of Freemasons.

The Celtic Gods

The Tuatha de Danaan were the people of the earth, the people of the goddess Dana, who once ruled Ireland until they were vanquished by the Milesians. At that point, they refused to leave Ireland, instead becoming the invisible race of fairies and elves, protected by their magical arts. They possessed four great treasures: the Stone of Destiny, the invincible sword of Nuada, the magic spear of Lugh, and the Cauldron of Dagda.

The Celtic gods are hard to pin down because, unlike the Greek, Roman, and Egyptian deities, their stories were never written down. They were passed on from tribe to tribe through oral tradition and migrated all over Pagan Britain with varying details. Still, all this makes for a rich folklore, if not an easy study.

Dana (Don, Ana, Danu) is mother of the gods, the Great Mother, goddess of plenty. As Brigit, she is patron of knowledge and poetry, patroness of women.

Dagda (Dagda Mor), father of the people of Dana, is a huge and powerful god who towers over the countryside. It is the Dagda who changes the seasons, summoning them with his harp. He owns a cauldron of plenty called Undry, from which he feeds the whole earth.

Angus, Dagda's son, is the bright and beautiful god of love. He is attended by four doves; when they sing, they arouse love in mortals, which is a lot nicer than shooting people with arrows, like Eros.

Midir, another son of Dagda, is the god of beauty.

Lir and his son **Manannan** are sea gods, although Manannan has eclipsed his father in popularity. The white crests of waves are his horses, so, like Neptune and Poseidon, he's also an equestrian god. Manannan guides the spirits of the dead to the Land of Youth, which lies beyond his ocean. He's also a trickster god who presides over illusions and magical objects: His cloak takes on a changing spectrum of colors, just as the sea does. The Isle of Man, named for him, is his home.

The Morrigan, or Morrigu, is actually three goddesses: the mother goddess Ana, the mother Babd, and the crone Macha. The Morrigan is also a goddess of war, who isn't shy about entering the battles herself in hand-to-hand combat. She haunts the battle-field in the form of a crow watching over the dead and making magic. Only the strongest and the most prepared should call on the Morrigan: Her worship is not for the faint of heart. She is another transformative goddess, who is quite capable of shaking your world to its foundations in order to strengthen you.

Brian or Bron is another giant god. He is the patron of minstrels and bards, and king of the underworld, where he guards the treasures of Dana.

Lugh is the god of light and the sun, master of the arts of war and peace. He wields the sword of Nuada that will fight his enemies all by itself, the magical spear of the Tuatha de Danaan, and a sling made of the rainbow.

Gwydion, a son of Dana, teaches the arts and poetry, and is also a great warrior. As a poet, he also has a soft spot for love. Gywdion is more often seen as a Welsh god, but he is strongly associated with the Tuatha de Danaan. When another Welsh son of Dana, **Lleu Llaw Gyffes** (sometimes associated with Lugh), was cursed to never have a wife from the people of the earth, the sympathetic Gwydion created a woman for him out of flowers.

The Gods of Egypt

There were hundreds of Egyptian deities, only a few of whom were prominent at any one time. This is partly because divinity was so entwined with political power. There were so many local gods that when a pharaoh took office, he or she usually elevated his or her local god to prominence. Also, the pharaoh was a living divinity, a strong link to the most powerful gods.

Much has been made of Pharaoh Cleopatra VII's marriages to Julius Caesar and later to Marcus Antonius, and while these may or may not have been love matches, they were certainly political. For either Caesar or Antony to hold power in Egypt, he would have had to marry the pharaoh (making him, by extension, a god, because Cleopatra, as ruler of Egypt, was considered divine) and she would have had to produce a child. Which she did, by Caesar and by Antony. Cleopatra may have been of Greek Macedonian lineage, but she was thoroughly Egyptian in her religious beliefs.

While religion heavily influenced the lives of Greeks, Romans, and Celts, it was absolutely everything to the Egyptians, governing all aspects of life and politics. Egyptian gods were unusual in that some were depicted as part human, part animal.

Isis and Osiris. The story of Isis, queen of the gods, and her husband Osiris is the bedrock of the Egyptian belief in death and rebirth. Osiris's brother, **Set,** god of storms, chaos, and trickery, was jealous of Osiris's power and his familial happiness. Under the guise of a celebration in his honor, Set managed to trick Osiris into lying down in a beautifully decorated sarcophagus, which Set then nailed shut and tossed into the Nile. He promptly ascended the throne of Egypt in Osiris's place. Isis managed to find the sarcophagus and hide it. When Set found out, he retrieved the body and cut it into pieces, which he hid all over the world. When Isis found out about this, she was, understandably, inconsolable, and she and her sister Nephthys searched all over the world for the body parts. She found everything but his penis; however, she had a new one, solid gold, made for him. Reassembling the pieces, she bathed the body in the healing waters of the Nile, which restored Osiris to life. As a result, Osiris is the god of the dead and of fertility and new life. Incidentally, in Egyptian art he is represented with a green face, green being the color of life. (Remember this at Halloween when the green-faced witches show up.) This story is so important because the Nile and its inundations were so crucial to Egyptian agriculture and survival. The reigning pharaoh held on to power partly because she or he was held to be Isis or Osiris on earth, and was held responsible for the inundations of the river. If the Nile flooded on a regular basis, depositing enough silt to grow crops, Pharaoh could sit secure on the throne. If not, he could start sending out his resumé. The famous Cleopatra VII, the one we're most familiar with, had this problem, which was the official excuse for her brother's attempt to depose her.

Horus, the son of Isis and Osiris. When Osiris entered the underworld as its ruler, Isis raised Horus in secrecy. Horus, as is usual with gods, vowed to avenge his father. He defeated Set but lost an eye in the process. Thoth gave him another eye, but the lost one, the Eye of Horus, the all-seeing protective Eye, became one of the most important symbols of Egypt, ranking right up there with the ankh of renewing life.

Anubis, the jackal-headed god, is the patron of embalming and the mummified dead, and is one of the most respected gods in the pantheon, probably because of the Egyptian beliefs about the afterlife and the survival of the soul. The goddess Maat weighs the hearts of the dead against the red feather of truth, but it is Anubis who sets the balance of the scales.

Maat is the goddess of justice and truth, who maintains balance in the universe and order in the natural world.

Hathor, the cow-headed goddess, is goddess of love, fertility, motherhood, and the joy of life, source of the Nile. She has a darker aspect, however, as Sekhmet, a lion-headed destroyer goddess.

Nut is the goddess of the night sky, most often depicted as arching over the world, wearing a star-spangled dress.

Thoth. When Maat weighs the soul, it is Thoth, the moon god, who records the results. He has the head of an ibis and is the patron of learning, writing, accounting, and wisdom.

Ra, the sun god. When the political power of Egypt shifted to Thebes, a local god, Amun, was combined with Ra and worshiped as Amun-Ra. Among Pagans of the more irreverent kind, there's a great chant to welcome the returning sun and summer: "He is the sun god, he is the fun god, Ra, Ra, Ra!" Its use in ancient Egypt is highly doubtful.

4

Coming Into Wicca

What attracts someone to Wicca?

The majority of newcomers fall into one of two categories. The first are people who are honestly looking for a spiritual experience and suspect that Wicca, with its rejection of a One True Male God as a creator and its basically unstructured, flexible form of worship, may be what they need. They may be just curious and it might never go anywhere from there, but they're serious about religion.

The second group—and there are way more of them—are just looking to shock or looking for a thrill. Oh, okay, there's more to it than that, but when you boil it down, it all reduces to "Notice me! I'm a rebel! I'm special!" They've heard that Wiccans cast spells and they like the possibility of magical control over any situation. They may have even attended a Wiccan Circle once and been impressed by the trappings: the crystal wands, the gilded chalice, the robes and jewelry, the candlelight—and they felt like this was *it*. To them, it's the outlaw version of the Catholic Church without all those pesky commandments. Some even believe that we're the ones with the black mass.

Remember this: *Being pissed off at your current religion is not a good reason to become a Wiccan.* If it was, we'd probably have more members than Regis Philbin has wrinkles.

Unfortunately, this reason pops up far more often than it should when we ask seekers why they're interested in Wicca. The often repeated story runs as follows, with very little variation: "I went to Catholic school and was the only one who suspected that what they were teaching about God and Jesus wasn't the whole truth, but when I questioned the nuns they resented my intelligence and they persecuted me. Oh yeah . . . and my grandmother was a Witch."

The really sad part of this is that it happens . . . well, except for the part about Granny. I'd consign my kid to almost any educational option except a church-run school, Catholic, Protestant, or any other religious flavor. If I wanted my child to learn religion, I'd teach her myself: School is for secular education.

Still, being dissatisfied with a particular religion is not a good reason to come to Wicca. It may be a good reason to *look into* Wicca, or to look into any other religion, but it isn't enough on which to base a commitment.

We get a lot of people like the Spiritual Shopper, too. She's definitely looking for the Blue Light Special of Religion. She's tried Catholicism, every flavor of Protestantism, a flirtation with Judaism, a little Buddhism, a little Sufi, Transcendental Meditation, crystal therapy, and Reiki. She's already been to Sedona, and she once spent a weekend on the Res with the shamans and emerged two days later as a Medicine Woman. On her list of New Age Options, the next item is Wicca. (Right after that is satanism—those guys are the absolute last on her list, but she doesn't want to be judgmental.) She's ruled out Voudoun, Macumba, and Santeria because the very idea of animal sacrifice makes her faint and she gets queasy around snakes. The cold fact is that this person isn't really interested in religion: She's interested in a trendy lifestyle, one that promises "personal enlightenment" so that she can finally understand her life, or fill it with something. Anything. She's afraid to be without *some* kind of religion.

Then there are the Dirty Old Men and Old Ladies (of every age) who only want to know what time the nekkid dancing in the woods starts, something I'd like to know myself. By the way, you know the difference between *naked* and *nekkid,* don't you? Naked is when you have no clothes on; nekkid is when you have no clothes on and you're up to something.

And don't even ask me about the people who show up in Salem every October with the fangs and the attitude. I always get the feeling that they're here only because they missed the last plane to New Orleans.

Okay, I've joked about these folks, but the majority of people who become interested in Wicca are really seeking *something.* They honestly feel some sort of void, and they're looking to fill the black hole that they see staring back at them.

The trouble is, most of them are not looking for religion. They're looking to belong. They want to be part of a special group or they want a family, preferably composed of "outsiders" like themselves who will create a power when together and protect them from the big bad world. They want to look down on what they refer to as the "mundane" world, the world that they think they've left behind. They'll go from group to group, looking for the perfect coven that will give them a sense of community, and they'll never find it.

This is the terrible problem with many who aspire to Wicca: They don't really *want* to live in the real world. They're actually looking for a fast escape into a small, artificially created atmosphere in which everyone is more or less like them. Hey, who isn't? That's why gated communities and country clubs and "ethnic neighborhoods" exist: so everyone can be just like everyone else and never come out of the wombs they've built, no matter how dysfunctional those wombs are. They're looking for a cult, but a cult of which they have a good chance of becoming the leader someday. Wicca, with its nonhierarchical structure and lack of central authority figures, seems to be exactly what they've been wanting for so long.

Generally, the same can be said of other groups, especially small religious sects. But it's also true of groups of people with specialized knowledge: Think of the MIS staff at most companies, the hard-core computer geeks who despise the rest of the workers, who feel that their computer skills make them special and above the crowd, and who only feel comfortable with others exactly like them. Not for nothing did *Saturday Night Live* feature an unpleasant character called "Nick Burns, Your Company's Computer Guy."

Wicca has its own set of special knowledge. The occult has had a fascination since the days of the cave people. As time went on, secret knowledge acquired a dangerous glamour with the rise of groups like the medieval alchemists, the Knights Templar, the Bavarian Illuminati, the Freemasons, the Theosophists, the Order of the Golden Dawn, and the more flamboyant of the Devil worshipers. Never mind that the real facts of some of these groups are wildly inflated (and the infighting among them sometimes as petty as the infighting among Witches): The legends endure. Even the Christian Church is founded on magical tales of a man who could raise the dead, turn water into wine, and who died and reappeared as a ghost. Catholic priests are supposed to be able to turn wine into blood.

Magic is the ultimate in special knowledge. Everyone wants to do it. And many people assume that becoming a Wiccan means automatically becoming a magician. They don't want to bother with religion: too much trouble, too many negative past associations, too much adherence to rules.

Many of these people would be much better off becoming ceremonial magicians, except that they don't want to do the work. Most seekers of magical knowledge aren't willing to wait to learn, and they certainly don't want to take months or years to do a single magical working.

Wicca sounds much easier to them, plus you get to wear cool

black capes and act and talk like you're living in a sanitized version of Merrye Olde Britain.

True Wiccans have a name for these people: "Insta-Witches." They want to read—at most—one or two books on Wicca, after which they expect to join a coven. Better yet, they spend a lot of time (and can spend a *lot* of money) finding a teacher. What they're looking for in a teacher is the same thing they experienced in school: They'll show up for class, ask a few questions and take a few notes, then, when the class is over, they want to take the exam and be initiated. They feel that they've done all the work they have to do. I've had some of these people in my classes. They're extremely competitive, trying to outdo the other students, asking completely off-the-subject questions designed to show how much more advanced they are than the others, and they're obsessed with getting past all this beginner stuff and getting on to the *real* secrets. Which, they assume, will only be revealed to the "top" students.

When I asked several experienced Wiccans what they know now that they didn't know when they first came to Wicca, many of them said, "How much work it is!" And that's on an ongoing basis. It never stops. In a lot of ways, you're always a student.

Insta-Witches don't want to hear this. They just want to buy all the stuff and start practicing with a coven so they can do "majick" or however they're spelling it this week.

What Is a Good Reason to Come Into Wicca?

There are a few. A love of the gods. A feeling of connection to divinity, or the desire to strengthen that connection, without the necessity of an intermediary. An instinctive rejection of the idea that there is only one true God and that one is male. A desire to worship the gods with others who also love those gods. An understanding that the connection with the gods can't be taught or proselytized, but must come from your own experience of them and willingness to listen to them in silence and solitude. A realization that this particular religion makes sense to you because of just those feelings, and no other religion lets you express them in just this way.

Any other reason and you're just playing witch.

Is Wicca a Cult?

Are you kidding? Wicca isn't organized enough to function as a cult, and we're certainly not organized enough to be a *dangerous* cult. We do have several cults of *personality*—that is, people who idolize this or that charismatic Wiccan leader or Big Name Pagan—but the rapidity with which this changes keeps Wicca from becoming another People's Temple. Individual Wiccans are too egotistical for that sort of behavior: Many of us don't mind being followers, but we strongly object to being slaves. Of course, there are exceptions, as we'll see in another chapter—naive or neurotic people who willingly follow self-styled leaders who only want to use them—but even these poor souls eventually wise up, even if only to find another manipulator.

Ironically, it's our idealism that saves us. We want our leaders to be perfect. When they show the slightest hint of being human, we're disillusioned and start looking for another hero. Tough for any potential Jim Joneses to develop a following long enough to brainwash anybody. Plus, Pagans would never be caught dead drinking Kool-Aid: They tend to prefer home-brewed mead, and the gods help anybody who tries to slip something into somebody's prized secret recipe.

I just said Wiccans are egotistical. This is one of those statements in which a perceived negative quality is turned into a positive one. One of the techniques used by cults is to destroy a person's sense of self-worth, so he or she will be easier to manipulate. When you think about it, the most refined examples of these techniques come from mainstream religions, which teach that man is nothing, man is miserable, sinful, low, and weak. And women are worse, tempting men (who are apparently too pinheaded to resist) into sin. Just look at the words of hymns, for instance, ". . . that saved a wretch like me . . ." According to these faithful, we're all lost lambs, strayed sheep, living in a world of woe until the glorious moment when we die and go to heaven, *provided* we've bought into the plan. God and Jesus are referred to as the Master, the Lord, the Almighty, the Savior of Mankind, the Father, which begs the question that if Jesus is the master, *somebody's* got to be the slaves. Guess who that is?

The emphasis on death as the supreme moment of life is what generally puts people off Christianity. Many Wiccans, like the ancient Pagans, see Christianity as a death cult, obsessed with symbols of death and suffering. And why not look forward to death, when all of life is seen as full of pitfalls leading to sin and damnation, something to be gotten through as quickly as possible so that you can die and thereby know *real* happiness? The only reason that more of these people don't kill themselves is that suicide is a sin and suffering is a virtue.

Wiccans simply don't have this mentality. Usually they've rejected those kinds of ideas long before they ever heard of Wicca.

Still, most Wiccans come from a Christian background, at least from a Christian-dominated society, and tend to carry those ideas into Wicca. A Jewish background isn't going to help you a whole lot, either, especially if you're female and buy into the Orthodox idea that you're "unclean" once a month, and that women who don't subordinate themselves to their husbands are courting disaster. The Hebrew legend of Lilith, the first wife of Adam, who rejected the superiority of man over woman and became demonized for it, looms large in the feminist branches of Wicca. When you've been exposed to these ideas since birth, when the principles behind them have become ingrained into a society, they stay with you no matter how far you try to distance yourself from them. Some feminist covens have transformed Lilith into a symbol for women's power, defying the stereotype, and her biggest supporters are the Jewish women and the Christians who are familiar with

Lilith's story. Definitely, Lilith got a raw deal. So did Jezebel, who was supposedly a priestess of Baal.

In mainstream religious society, the priests, rabbis, and ministers are the learned, superior beings who alone are capable of interpreting the Word o' God. This is an old, old carryover from the days when education, and even the ability to read, was reserved for the priests. It was a means of establishing control and, in a way, it still is: We have an image of a priest, priestess, pastor, or rabbi possessing wisdom or enlightenment that the rest of us don't. People can read theology for themselves, but we still look to the church authority figure as just a little wiser than we are by virtue of his or her having some kind of ordained education. Also, in American society, we have a superstitious but deeply ingrained respect for the professional, and what is a priest, priestess, pastor, or rabbi but a professional religious person? It's slightly illogical, because we've all known professional people who didn't know their ass from their elbow about their own professions, but there you are: We still expect them to know more than the rest of us. We expect—and we have every right to expect it—that the words *ordained* or *initiated* equate with a higher level of knowledge.

Historically, the congregations in mainstream religion are the unenlightened, sinful sheep who must be led along to the glorious afterlife by means of regular church or temple attendance and strict adherence to the rules. If you fall off the salvation wagon, you can repent your sins, make amends, get saved, and climb right back on. Some backsliding is expected because, after all, you're simply a lost lamb. In fact, the backsliding helps. If you, a miserable sinner, revert to your evil ways and get in real trouble, and then you're forgiven, you'll be that much more grateful, that much more in spiritual debt, and less likely to question those who forgave you. It's a really neat trick.

This early religious and social conditioning always kicks in when someone considers coming to Wicca. It's very difficult for people to accept a religion that tells you that you're responsible for your own spiritual development, and that if you screw up, nobody's going to offer you Instant Forgiveness so that all your transgressions will be wiped away. One of the almost universal beliefs of Wicca is that of karma: It's the governing force behind personal responsibility, that what we do and are and will become is based on our choices.

Another problem for newcomers is that we have no bibles or scriptures to interpret. If the gods (as is more usual) want to tell you something, they'll tell you directly with no intervention. It's your responsibility to listen. If you choose to disregard the gods, it's your ass.

To some extent, even longtime practicing Wiccans exhibit some of the characteristics of cult members. They're more comfortable hanging out with other Wiccans, speaking in words or phrases that are meaningless to those outside the religion. There are code words for those outsiders: *cowans, mundanes,* even that holdover from the hippie days of the 1960s: *straights.* And since the advent of Harry Potter, some Wiccans are even using the term *muggles.*

The more that a Wiccan lives exclusively in a Wiccan or Pagan community, the more pronounced is his or her alienation from non-Pagan society. This is especially true of the Wiccan who has dropped out of the usual working world, those who are on some kind of public assistance, or who work in strictly Pagan-oriented businesses such as Witch stores or as professional readers. Their whole orientation is toward Wicca or Witchcraft; they have very little else to talk about, and very few friends outside the Pagan world.

In Salem we've seen many, many people who have come here strictly to live in what they expect will be a "Witch community" where everyone wears ceremonial robes all the time and we're all one big happy laughing coven, attending Circles every full moon and big celebrations with dancing in the streets on the Sabbats and, probably, Saturday Afternoon Wiccan Ice Cream Socials. It just doesn't happen. And when they see that it doesn't, they get very bitter. They're not what you'd call self-starters: they're expecting someone else, someone *in charge,* to take responsibility for *their* spiritual well-being, to organize Circles or events for them to attend, to create the perfect coven or group for them to join. They rarely think of creating that reality themselves. They're too conditioned to some spiritual leader arranging everything, to being spoon-fed their religion. Ironically, if someone does step up to the plate to arrange things, most of these people criticize the result because it isn't what they envisioned.

What Really Happens in Wicca?

Each Wiccan is responsible for his or her own religious experience. This is a religion based on your own relationship with the gods, with no intermediary, and that means that you're on your own.

Even if you're part of an oathbound, by-the-book Trad such as the Gardnerians, you're still expected to get in touch with and develop your own power, and your own connection with divinity.

And when that happens, you know it. You stand in a Circle, by yourself or with others, and you feel a real communion with the gods; you feel your life change, perhaps in a small way, but you feel it. There's no "maybe" there. This is the essence of the Mysteries, the one true secret of Wicca.

What Happens in Circles, What Doesn't, and What Shouldn't

Maybe it's me, but it's very difficult for me to feel any real power from most public Circles, which is why I no longer attend them. Public Circles are usually very large and very theatrical, with every detail worked out in advance. There's no room for anything spontaneous: If the gods had anything special to say, they'd have to set the place on fire in order to get noticed.

In Salem, Circles almost never start on time: The presiding priest and priestess sometimes show up as much as an hour to two hours late, a sign that they have very little respect for the people gathered there. This isn't a Salem phenomenon: The concept of "Pagan Standard Time" is something the entire Wiccan world should toss overboard immediately. When things finally do get under way, the people are expected to stand during the interminable casting of the Circle, cleansing, casting out of "negativity" (of which there's plenty, considering how long people have been waiting), the long ceremonial calling of the quarters, the singing of the bards, and all the following ritual. I maintain that the gods don't care if you're standing, sitting, or lying down as long as you're there and truly engaged. But there's nothing to get involved *with:* Public Circles are structured so that the priests and acolytes are very busy, but the "congregation" has almost nothing to do. They're just the audience, there to appreciate the show. At one Beltane Circle there was a nice Maypole, but only members of the initiated Inner Circle were allowed to dance around it.

The priestess and priest at the last Circle I attended looked and acted as if they'd done this so many times that they were just going through the motions. But they dutifully went through with it because the ordinary people expected the "celebrity Pagans" to preside. It seemed to me that if they'd been really excited about conducting a Circle, or at least enjoyed it and looked forward to the experience, they'd have been on time.

Let me add a quick note here. *If you're a priest or priestess who gets bored presiding at a Circle, or you're not up for it, or you just don't feel that connection, maybe you should appoint somebody or ask for a volunteer to take your place.* Wicca is supposed to be a religion in which all of us are priestesses and priests, all able to conduct the rites. Surely, in a coven or group large enough to be holding big public Circles, you can find at least one other initiated person capable of the duties. If you can't, then there's a deeper problem, either with the way you train and initiate, or with the ego of the clergy involved.

After several of these circuses, I stopped attending. I certainly wasn't contributing any energy, which does nobody any good, not that there was anything to contribute *to.* I felt that the group could have gotten together for a good Wiccan party and raised a lot more energy besides having a really good time meeting people.

In another public Circle conducted by a different group, the attendees were instructed to "direct all your energy into the priestess," who was performing a healing. What the . . . ? What did she need *our* energy for? Couldn't she muster any on her own? *She* was the one who was supposed to be drawing down the moon and directing energy to everyone else. That's the priestess's job. And many of us didn't know this woman all that well, at least not well enough to take the karmic hit for her if she turned out not to know what she was doing. Better to have directed our healing energy directly toward the sick person, in our own way.

I've got to say, though, that the success or failure of a public Circle depends on the "public" part. I attended a very elaborate and very large Circle at a Wiccan weekend gathering in Dallas where I was a guest speaker. This Circle even had a professional *choreographer*. The resulting power practically knocked you over. The difference was that, although this was a big group comprised of a lot of covens, almost all of them knew each other. Plus, they were all excited about holding the Circle in the first place. And the choreographer really helped, because everyone was involved in some way, especially in the dancing, which he made very simple to follow and exhilarating without being strenuous. Nobody was just a spectator. Everything went smoothly.

Everything but me, that is. They had asked me to call the Eastern quarter. So the Circle was cast and the quarters were supposed to be called and everyone just stood there waiting, me included, until the priest whispered, "That's *you*, honey!"

Oopsie. In my own Trad, we always started calling the quarters with North; I'd forgotten that practically the rest of the entire Wiccan world starts with East. So I had been politely standing there wondering why whoever was calling the energies of the North wasn't on the old spiritual ball, and waiting to do my stuff with the Powers of the Air.

Most private Circles I've attended have been astounding. People were there not only to honor the gods, but to communicate with them and to raise energy to solve problems. This is something you just can't do in a very large public Circle where people either don't know each other or know only a few of the people involved.

I've always felt a little uncomfortable with drawing down the moon or drawing the energy of the gods into myself as a priestess acting for a group, even for my own coven. I'm very, very happy with what's happening to *me personally* during those moments, but I was never quite sure how that was going to benefit everyone else. The basic idea is that the priestess directs the energy out, or speaks for the Goddess. That's true, and that's what happens usually, although you can't force the gods to attend. But it always seemed to me to be too much like mainstream religion, where the minister is hearing the Word o' Gawd and interpreting it for the lowly peasants. If I was conducting Circles now as a priestess, I'd revise the rituals so that everyone is performing the drawing or the rite at once, privately calling on the particular gods whom they love the most, or whom they need at the time, and give them some quiet meditation time to talk with the deity.

Speaking of meditation, I'm a bit wary of Circles that go in for long guided meditations or inner shamanic journeys under the guidance of the priest or priestess. Most priestesses and priests are not therapists or psychologists and are not trained to handle the problems that might come bubbling up out of someone's psyche. To do this kind of thing in public Circles, or even private Circles where there are some participants you don't know well, is asking for trouble. As for the type of guided meditations that are interminable nonstop narrated trips into Fantasyland, with every detail of every fairy ring and soft rain and warm breeze spelled out for you, during which you are supposed to receive a message from the gods—*arrgggghh*. If the gods had something to say to you, how are you supposed to hear it over all that chattering? Frankly, after about two minutes of this, my mind just blanks out with boredom. After ten minutes, my butt gets numb.

In a really effective Circle, the priestess and priest are not only the representatives of the Goddess and the God but also function as the spiritual coordinators, making sure that everything happens in a certain order so that the participants don't have to concern themselves with the details and can concentrate on the revelatory spiritual experience. They also make sure that things run smoothly and don't descend into chaos.

Unless you're a Discordian, in which case, you're supposed to be actively encouraging that sort of thing.

5

Learning Wicca

A BEGINNER'S CHAPTER

The best way to learn about Wicca is to read about it.

Sorry . . . the second best way. The best is if someone in your family is a Wiccan and teaches you. Even then, you'd probably be learning only one way, or one Tradition, out of many possibilities. So I guess I was right the first time. *That* doesn't happen often.

I'm going to tell you this right up front: Do yourself a favor and read Ronald Hutton's *The Triumph of the Moon* right away. It's going to save you a lot of confusion later when you're trying to sort out the real claims for Wicca from the bogus, and you'll find yourself referring to it often. Hutton has done a superb job of pulling together all the legitimate scholarship concerning Wicca, and has added his own work, and there's no better overview of the history of the religion. His historical emphasis is strongly British, as he admits, but since Wicca in America was an import in the first place, the book is no less useful for it. Frankly, reading this book will save you a lot of money in the long run: It will help you evaluate the authenticity of the claims of some other writers on Wicca, so that you can judge which books contain real information. Not that Hutton's book is a standard against which all books should be measured: No book is, but it does put a lot of what we accept about Wicca into perspective.

It isn't as if it's hard to find a book on Wicca: Since the adoption of the religion in the United States, in the early 1960s, the books have been proliferating like bunnies. Some people are of the opinion that there are way too many books out there, and to those people I say: *Hey, go watch some more TV reruns.* The more books, the better chances there are of people finding exactly what they need. There's almost no aspect of Wicca that hasn't been covered in at least one book and more likely in dozens.

Gone are the days when you'd have to scrounge all over to find a New Age, Pagan, or Wiccan bookshop: Every big city's got at least one, and so do plenty of smaller towns. If you're from a really small town in the Bible Belt, you've still got the Internet, and lots of small booksellers have Web sites. (I like small booksellers and try to support them when I can.) I even found a Wiccan store in Nashville, Tennessee. Nashville calls itself the Buckle of the Bible Belt, and for good reason, so to be an out-of-the-closet Wiccan there takes real guts.

All the big chain bookstores have a New Age section: It's just good business, with growing numbers of people looking for these books. Yeah, the fundamentalists try to get them to stop carrying Wiccan and Pagan titles, but as long as people are buying them, it just ain't gonna happen.

So there you are, standing in front of shelves crammed with Wicca books and finding yourself very confused.

How do you know which books are good?

Well, you bought *this* one, so what more do you need?

Kidding! Really! Kind of.

The best way is to just stand there and browse through a few. Take a pile of them and sit down on the floor to skim through them, if you have to. Pay no attention to the possible dirty looks of the clerks in the big chains: You're entitled to have a good look before you buy. Just put 'em back where you found them when you're through. Scan the table of contents and read the introduction or the first chapter. The intro should tell you a little about the book, the author's reason for writing it, and what he or she hopes to accomplish with it.

If the author tells you that this is the only book you'll ever need, forget it. No one book on Wicca is all you'll ever need. The diversity within the religion is too rich and too crammed with personal experience to be covered by one author.

When you're just starting out, you need some good how-to-do-it Wicca books, like Scott Cunningham's *Wicca for the Solitary Practitioner* and Starhawk's *The Spiral Dance*. And don't pay any attention to the people who have been Wiccans for years who'll tell you that Cunningham's books are too simple: These folks conveniently forget how lost *they* were when they started out. Everyone has his or her own list of favorite books, but you also have to choose the books that sound right to you, a very personal choice.

Doing a lot of reading now may save you some grief in the future, when you may be choosing a teacher or a coven. I hate to say it, but there are indeed opportunists out there who are looking for raw beginners who haven't read a thing. And there are high priestesses and priests who only know their own Trads and can't give you a very broad magical education. Then you've got those people who set themselves up as high priests or priestesses after reading one book and then founding a coven or Trad consisting only of themselves and a couple of students. Some people know what they're doing, some don't. If you've read a lot, you'll know enough to be able to sort them out.

As we've already discussed, don't forget to head over to the shelves of history, anthropology, social sciences, and books on the histories of other religions. Read a lot of mythology: Greek, Roman, Celtic, Germanic, Egyptian. And don't forget to read Joseph Campbell. All of these will really help.

Study Groups

I can't say enough good things about study groups. These are made up of people who have come together in an informal atmosphere to share information. Sometimes there'll be book reports, sometimes just discussion or a mixture of the two. Each study group sets its own agenda.

A good study group isn't a coven and isn't limited to one area of study. Depending on how many people are in it, a study group can consist of people studying Wicca, Witchcraft, magic, the history of Pagan religions—almost anything, whatever the group members are interested in. Some groups like to limit themselves to one area: Wicca, for instance. But the more varied your reading, the more informed you'll be.

Occasionally, a study group will turn into a coven, or just start holding Circles, if the members get along and share the same points of view. But don't make this your objective.

The best groups, in my opinion, are the ones where everyone is at about the same level of experience and no one attempts to manipulate the group because he or she has read more books or once met some Celebrity Witch at a Pagan gathering. When everyone starts out more or less the same, it's really exciting after a few months when you realize how much you've learned. And you will learn: It's unavoidable.

Don't think that study groups are always all sweetness and light. Like all other groups of various people, study groups can contain some bad apples or just pain-in-the-butt people. But unlike covens or more formal groups, there usually aren't a lot of politics because there's no position to jockey for. There's no high priestess, no president or elected officers. There might be someone who arranges the meeting place or the schedule, but that's no big deal. Generally, if someone decides he wants to run the group, he'll just start his own. Leaving a study group doesn't involve breaking any oaths or violating any secrecy. You're just there to comment on the books you've been reading. If you don't like the group, leave. There is, or should be, no commitment to a study group.

Some study groups like to really get into it, doing written book reports and having assigned readings, meetings, and topics scheduled months ahead, along with recommended book lists. If you like that structure, set it up that way. Some groups just like to meet because they don't want to feel alone in their interests. Which, frankly, is the reason that many covens have started.

Special note for teens: Study groups really make sense for you because you can work with people close to your own age and level of experience. Unfortunately, you'll find that a lot of adult groups don't want to work with teens. This isn't because of prejudice; it's a legal issue. There's nothing illegal or immoral about what you'd be learning in a good adult study group or coven, but it's happened too often that parents—often parents who have never, up to that point, bothered to find out who their kids associate with or what they do, much less take an interest in the kids' spiritual needs—suddenly decide that these heathens are probably trying to recruit their kids into some kind of cult. You can imagine the resulting legal nightmares. That's why adult covens and groups rarely take in anyone under legal age, usually eighteen, and if they make an exception, many require written consent from the parents or guardians, handed over in person, not sent along with the minor, sometimes notarized. But most adult groups won't take kids under any circumstances, unless the minor is the child of a coven member. Also, it's less risky for you to work with other kids. Although Wiccans indignantly protest that it never happens, there are some adults who see teen newcomers as easy to control. This isn't limited to Wicca; as we've read in too many headlines, other religions have problems with ministers or youth group leaders taking advantage of kids and teens. Working in a group of kids your own age is safer, and will actually be more satisfying for you. You're taking responsibility for your own spirituality—a big step, even for adults. It's fun when you start out knowing nothing, then look back a few months later and realize how far you've come on your own.

Finding a Study Group

It's easier to form a group than to find one, because not all groups advertise or announce themselves. Groups that have come together spontaneously are more common than those that have advertised for members. But if you have a Wiccan, Pagan, or New Age shop in your town, that's a good place to ask about existing groups. If the shop has a bulletin board, various groups may have put up notices stating that they're accepting new members. Also, talk with the shop's staff or the owner: These folks tend to keep up with what's going on in town.

Try the Internet. The Witches' Voice at www.witchvox.com, Beliefnet at www.beliefnet.com, and the Witches' League for Public Awareness at www.celticcrow.com all have state-by-state listings of groups and covens, with contact information.

The latest, and one of the best, trends are Pagan-oriented community centers—meeting places that are "nondenominational" and open to Wiccans, Witches, and Pagans of all beliefs. If you live in the Dallas area, I recommend that you head right over to Betwixt and Between, the interfaith community center, with a strong Pagan emphasis. It offers public Circles, plus excellent and imaginative programs and activities, some purely for fun. They even have a cafe! If your town has a community center, support it if you use it, preferably with donations: These places are nonprofits, and many have astoundingly high overheads for rent and utilities.

Unitarian Universalist Pagans

If your town has a Unitarian church, ask them if they have a CUUPs group, the Covenant of the Unitarian Universalist Pagans. This group, part of the Unitarian Universalist Association of Congregations, provides networking and education, develops liturgy and theology, and is an excellent way to meet other Wiccans and Pagans. Most of the people are from various Trads and backgrounds. If I was moving to a new town, I'd look up the local CUUPs group right away, especially if I didn't know anyone. Many Pagans have gravitated to the Unitarian Universalists: Member congregations are required to be noncreedal, which means that they don't require specific beliefs. Within a single UU congrega-tion, you'll find atheism, Humanism, liberal Christianity, Buddhism, Judaism, and Paganism. Needless to say, a UU congregation is an interesting place to discover new ideas.

Many CUUPs chapters have study groups or even formal lec-ture series. The one in Salem is very busy, providing wonderful speakers and even concerts of Pagan musicians.

Forming a Study Group

Put up your own notice in the local Pagan shops, or maybe on your public library bulletin board. If you don't mind casting a wide net, you might run a small ad in the personals classified ads of the local paper. You can have people contact you at a post office or commercial box number. If you want to interview people by phone, you're going to have to give your phone number. And there's always e-mail: If you don't want to use your regular e-mail account, there are hundreds of sites like Yahoo and Hotmail offering free e-mail accounts.

If you're a teen, you can put the word out at school, or ask only those people whom you feel have the same interest in Wicca that you do. This is the safest way to do it. If you're using the methods men-tioned above, I just want to remind you of what you probably already know: Watch out for the loonies who prey on kids and teens. You know those sick pedos like to haunt the Internet, pretending to be kids and urging kids to meet them somewhere. I'd advise you to stick with asking your friends and kids you know.

First you have to find a place to meet. If you've put up a notice at a local Pagan shop, or if you've run an ad in the papers and you're going to be meeting strangers, you do not want them to come to your home until you know more about them. Frankly, you're going to run into at least one unpleasant person; I can guarantee it. I can also guarantee that you're going to be pestered by religious fundie nutcases who live to harass Wiccans and Pagans and will scream Bible verses over the phone or send religious tracts by mail. I once had some wacko read the entire Catholic Rite of Exorcism into my answering machine, which was interesting but was . . . oh, what's the word? . . . oh yeah: *stupid*. Don't even ask what these jerks will do to your e-mail account. If I was a betting woman, I'd lay odds on your also meeting at least one of the following:

- The dirty old man who's heard that all Pagans run nekkid in the woods and just can't wait to get in on it.
- The dirty young man who's looking to get laid and has heard that Pagans are into group sex.
- Some druggie who wants to rationalize getting wasted as a spiritual "altered state of consciousness" or a "shamanic experience."
- The guy who wants to learn "magick" because he hopes that he (almost always a "he") can use it to control others.
- The needy neurotic (almost always a "she") who speaks mainly in psychobabble, has tried every form of therapy, and has now "given herself permission" to use Wicca to "find a spiritual family" in which her "inner child" will "feel safe" and into which she will dump all her seismic emotional upheavals, then throw a *grand mal* tantrum when the group turns out not to be a solution to her problems.

A coffee shop or fast-food place makes a good place to interview prospective group members (you can make a fast getaway at Mickey D's, *plus* get a burger). Trust your instincts, and remember that sociopaths are almost always charming—at first.

Finding a Meeting Place

The local church is probably going to turn you down if you ask to meet there. Unless it's a Unitarian Universalist congregation.

Ideally, until the group members get to know each other well enough to rotate meetings at each other's homes, you need a neutral meeting place. Try your local library. If your group isn't big, the library sometimes has meeting or study rooms available, and you can reserve them in advance. So do some local museums.

Some coffee shops or restaurants have large private rooms that you can use as long as everyone orders lunch or dinner. Not a bad idea—a steak with baked potato *and* spiritual enlightenment.

Also check community centers to see if they have meeting space. Even places like the Red Cross or some schools or universities might have rooms you can use. You may have to pay a fee for these, but they won't usually be expensive.

If you're meeting in the spring or summer, look into meeting at local parks. In Salem, we have two terrific parks, one with covered pavilions that are first-come, first-serve. You can put up a bunch of colored balloons so everyone can find the spot. Some parks even have indoor meeting places that can be reserved: Call your town park service and find out.

Since you're meeting at a public place, it's a good idea to tell everyone not to wear fancy robes or black T-shirts with foot-high pentacles printed in Day-Glo. I know it shouldn't matter, but it does. Also, this is a *study group:* Don't try to make it into a full-blown event by holding a Circle complete with incense and candles at the meetings. Otherwise, what will happen is that, at the very least, you'll worry the proprietors, and you'll probably get nosy onlookers peeking constantly in the door "just to see what's going on!" Your objective is to find a quiet, neutral place to meet, not to cause a disruption of the meeting place's normal business.

I used to teach classes in a business meeting room at a local hotel, and I asked for donations to pay for the room, because I wasn't charging anything for the class. Since the classes usually averaged about twenty people and we met at night, it was hard to find a large enough space anywhere else. (Our town library closed at five o'clock. Damn those funding cuts!) If you have to pay for a space, be sure to let everyone know it up front, and ask them to kick in for the cost.

When you're reserving spaces and people ask you what for, you don't have to jump right up and say, "A study group for Witch-craft!" Do that, and you're likely to be met with a skeptical or even hostile look. You're then going to have to go through a long and pointless explanation of what a Witch is and isn't. During that long explanation, people aren't even going to hear you because they've already made up their minds that you're a flake.

What's wrong with saying you need space for a spirituality study group, or a book or readers club, or a historical or folkloric study group? Those all apply to your study. Most people just want to know you're not running a how-to workshop on building nu-clear weapons or synthesizing designer drugs in their space. Your objective is to find a space to use on a regular basis, not to educate the world on Wicca. Not yet. When you know enough about it yourself and can discuss it intelligently—get yourself an audience and do us all some good!

If you're a teen, the best place to have a study group is at your home, or the home of one of the study group members, with parents in the house. Also, if your school provides a meeting place for after-school activities for other religious groups, they're supposed to pro-vide one for Wiccan kids, too. Otherwise, they're practicing religious discrimination. I say they're "supposed to," because many schools don't realize that Wicca is a religion that comes under equal protec-tion of the law according to the First Amendment. You could still have a very hard time getting your school to let you meet, probably harder than you bargained for, so if they say no and you and your parents aren't prepared for a bout in the courts, try to find another meeting place. If your group is small, your local library is a better bet.

Finding and Evaluating a Teacher

When someone becomes interested in Wicca, almost invariably she starts looking for a teacher. As we've seen, this isn't the best first step, because beginners have no idea what constitutes a good teacher, or how to evaluate the material that's being taught.

If you've got a specific Tradition in mind—you know you want to be, for instance, a Gardnerian Wiccan—then you're going to need to find a Gardnerian coven and let them train you. Just realize that you'll be learning only the Gardnerian way of doing things. If you decide one day that it isn't for you, you're going to have to start over with whatever Trad you're moving to. And many Traditions require at least a year and a day to complete the initial study. If you're working with a Trad with a degree system, it takes at least a year and a day to work toward each degree.

Before you decide to make such a commitment, be sure you want to study that particular Trad. And you can't know that until you've gathered some information on it, preferably in contrast to other Trads or ways of practicing Wicca. The best way to be informed is to familiarize yourself with many Trads, then find out more specifics on the ones that most closely match your spiritual goals. (See chapter 6, on Traditions.) Read some books, or go on the Internet: You'll find hundreds of Web sites from hundreds of covens of almost every known Trad.

Once you've decided on a Trad or a group, you need to evaluate the material you're going to be taught, and the person teaching it.

This is the really tricky part, and this is where your reading experience will help guide you. Ask to look over the class materials, or request an outline of what will be taught. Ask to see the recommended reading list for the class. If you're studying with a coven, they'll usually have a list of required readings for initiation candidates. Find out everything you can before you begin.

Ask for the credentials of the person who'll be teaching. If you're taking a class with a Big Name Pagan, find out if the BNP is going to be doing the actual teaching or is just lending his or her name to the enterprise.

Credentials are sticky, because Wicca doesn't have any divinity schools that train ministers or teachers. The closest things we have are groups like the Cherry Hill Seminary and the Covenant of the Goddess.

Cherry Hill is interesting. They seem to have a real commitment to effective training of Wiccan clergy, and their course list is impressive. The instructors include Cat Chapin-Bishop, Judy Harrow, and M. Macha NightMare, people who have earned respect in the Wiccan communities. You can go to the Cherry Hill Web page and get more information: www.cherryhillseminary.org.

The Covenant of the Goddess has been around since 1975, representing the interests of Wiccans, and is now a huge international organization with hundreds of member covens. They ordain ministers who have met their established criteria. Find out more at www.cog.org.

Wicca by Mail

I've never taken a Wiccan correspondence course, but like most Wiccans who have been practicing a while, I'm familiar with the two schools that have been around the longest. Because I haven't taken the courses myself, I can't tell you whether they're good, bad, or mediocre, but I do know the people who run both schools and can definitely say that they're devout practitioners of the religion. As for the courses, you should look at the schools' Web sites, e-mail them for more info if you have any questions, and find out for yourself before you make a commitment.

The Church and School of Wicca, run by Gavin and Yvonne Frost, who have been practicing and teaching since 1968, was the first correspondence school to teach Wicca, and it's the best known. They claim to have taught thousands of students, and there's no reason to doubt it. You can study everything from beginning Wicca to Astral Travel, and the courses contain lots of material. They're at www.wicca.org.

Our Lady of Enchantment has been around for twenty years, teaching by mail order, and claims twenty-five thousand students. This school is run by Lady Sabrina, a longtime Witch in New Hampshire. If you live in New England, you're always invited to drop by the Our Lady of Enchantment events. The Web page is http://members.aol.com/LadyS1366/oloe.html.

6

Traditions

HOW WICCANS DO WHATEVER IT IS THEY'RE DOING

> I am a particularly haughty and exclusive person . . . I
> can trace my ancestry back to a protoplasmic primordial
> atomic globule. Consequently, my family pride is
> something inconceivable.
>> Pooh Bah in *The Mikado,* Gilbert and Sullivan

Early Influences: When Gerry Met Crowley

In the beginning, there was the Word, and the Word came from
Gerald Gardner. Or so the story goes. There's been more argument
over whether Wicca originated with Gardner than there has been
debate over when life actually begins. The contention seems to be
over how much of Wicca Gardner made up and how much, if any,
consisted of remnants of authentic Pagan practices.

Whatever.

It hardly makes a difference now, because the machinery that
Gardner set in motion has taken on a momentum independent of
him. There will always be those who claim that every word Gardner spoke was truth, and those who claim that he was a charlatan,
plus all shades of opinion in the middle. This is pretty standard
stuff for those who publicly practice magic and garner a lot of
publicity about it: There'll always be a host of rival magicians
clamoring to discredit each other and—incidentally—promote
themselves. Personally, I like the theory that he was an occultist
and a dirty old man who included skyclad rituals so he could be
spanked by naked women. It's just so . . . *English.*

No matter what brand of Wicca you're practicing, it's very likely that you're using some form of the rituals and beliefs set forth by Gardner. I've seen vocal anti-Gardnerians hold rituals that included casting a Circle, reading from a Book of Shadows, using an athame, and calling the Elements or Watchtowers, all of which were herded into Wicca by Gardner. And the majority of Wiccans are not only using the elements that Gardner collected, they're using them in much the same manner. True, most of what Gardner put together as Wicca can be found in other, earlier sources, but you can't deny that Gardner did a lot of homework by shaping it all into a coherent (mostly) system. As much as Wiccans like to claim individuality, they're never very far from Gardner, like him or not. Most of them haven't read the earlier sources, such as various studies on ceremonial magic, Kabbalah, and the histories of various occult groups; if they have, it's usually because they were first introduced to these sources by practicing what Gardner preached.

The truth is that there's almost no occult or magical group that doesn't owe something to the groups preceding it. No matter how exalted-sounding the practices of the group, it's for sure that the founders filched either more or less of their beliefs, rituals, oaths, tools or other metaphysical trappings from somebody else. You can go back pretty far in history—to Greece, Rome, Egypt, Mesopotamia—and not find one group that hasn't adapted something from some other group or culture. When it comes to religion, everybody's a protestant: They all broke off from some group and formed another one more to their taste. The most famous protestant of them all was Jesus, who, like many of us, had some ethical doubts about his previous religion.

Gardner was fortunate in that he was studying magic during one of those periods of history when occultism and mysticism were all the rage. There have been many such periods, usually coming toward the end of a century or just before or after devastating social upheavals, like major wars. One of the most fruitful of these times was the late eighteenth century, when the great magicians like the Comte de St-Germain and Allessandro di Cagli-ostro thrilled the crowds of decadent aristos. St-Germain's reputation remained pretty much intact, enough of his mysterious glamour surviving so that a modern group of end-of-the-worlders led by Elizabeth Claire Prophet (the Church Universal and Triumphant) still regard him as a patron saint. Cagliostro was later discredited, but his influence during his time was enormous. And Cagliostro, like others who came later, knew his magical traditions. His rituals, like Wicca, incorporated a little of everything: Kabbalah, Freemasonry, alchemy, early Roman and Etruscan rites, the Eleusinian Mysteries, the Orphic Mysteries, and the Egyptian rites, which themselves were adapted from Mesopotamian magic. A veritable Chinese menu of high magic.

Another period of magical interest, and one of the most spectacular, came in the mid- to late 1800s and lasted (although diminished) into the early years before World War I. Those years saw the heyday of Theosophy, the Golden Dawn, the Rosicrucians, the Spiritualists, the Stella Matutina, the Fraternity of the Inner Light, a strong resurgence of the Masonic Order, Co-Masonry (which admitted women to the Mysteries: Gardner was a Co-Mason), and other magical and occult societies. The personalities were colorful and highly visible: Helena Blavatsky, Annie Besant, MacGregor Mathers, Frances Farr, Eliphas Levi, A. E. Waite, William Butler Yeats, Dion Fortune, and the greatest occult showman since Cagliostro and Casanova: Aleister Crowley. Lest you assume that Witch Wars are a modern phenomenon, you should study the soap-opera goings-on between some of these drama-queen magi. My favorite was the argument between Crowley and MacGregor Mathers of the Hermetic Order of the Golden Dawn: They were throwing curses, demons, and vampires at each other. Apparently, every day was a party back in the great occult revival days.

Gardner got in on the tail end of all this—he was born in 1883—but there was enough of it still around during the 1930s and 1940s that he could get a good grounding in occult study:

Dion Fortune founded the Fraternity of the Inner Light in 1924; several splinter groups of the Golden Dawn were still going strong; the Rosicrucians . . . who knew what *they* were doing, because they'd been surfacing and disappearing since the founder, Christian Rosenkreutz, was supposedly working miracles in the fourteenth century. And the most famous and scandalous of the high magicians was Aleister Crowley.

By the time Gardner met him, Crowley was drawing close to death, sunk into poverty and physically devastated by long years of alcohol and drug use, but his mind seemed as sharp as ever. Crowley had been booted out of more distinguished groups than most of us could ever dream of entering. He had a little problem with leadership—if it wasn't his, he got impatient. He was smart, and quick to absorb the basic principles of these societies, and eventually put together his first group, Argentium Astrum, by cadging bits here and there and adding his own research and opinions. Not too different from the methods of today's Wicca, actually. And not so different from Christianity, itself a pastiche of earlier religions and mythologies.

Gardner's meeting with the notorious Crowley was apparently a revelation for Gardner, an Aleister groupie from way back. But here's where all the controversy comes in: How much of his growing ideas of Wicca did Gardner get from Crowley? How much did he take from the New Forest Coven, the secret group of Witches that supposedly initiated him? How much did pop anthropologist Margaret Murray influence his work (actually, that seemed like a quid pro quo deal: Both of them made the most of their association). What parts of Wicca are from the Golden Dawn, the Rosicrucians, other ceremonial magic groups, various other sources, and Gardner's own research?

These questions have been driving Wiccans nuts ever since Gardner made his predilections public in 1951 by publishing *Witchcraft Today.* I think the chances for resolving them are about the same as selling the pope on Scientology. Too much time has passed, and most of the answers wouldn't make any difference in the actual practice of Wicca anyway. It's too ingrained now. More than fifty years have gone by since Gardner became the most famous out-of-the-closet Witch in the world, and Wicca is still evolving and growing, with devoted followers of various Traditions who have been practicing and training others for all that time. A sudden discovery that the Gardnerian Book of Shadows is completely authentic or that Gardner made up the whole thing just to win a bar bet probably wouldn't change a thing, even among the Gardnerians themselves.

If you want to learn the source of many of the elements that make up Gardnerian Wicca, read a good book on the Masonic rites. You'll find a lot there that's very familiar. I like John Robinson's *Born in Blood: The Lost Secrets of Freemasonry.* You can skip the first half of the book, in which Robinson traces the probable origins of the Masons back to the Knights Templar and the medieval guilds, and get right to the second half, which goes deeply into the rituals, oaths, and initiation rites of the Masons. If you've been a Wiccan for a while, be prepared for a real sensation of déjà vu. The oaths, the Old Charges, the initiation rites (in which the candidate can have no metal on his or her body, among other familiar requirements), the degree system, and the reference to Freemasonry as "the Craft" are among the most prominent of the similarities.

Tradition is the word used for the variations on Wiccan practice—the systems, beliefs, and rituals of different groups. To list every Trad would be a book in itself, probably running to several volumes, and most of those would be useless, since almost all Trads share more or less common features. There are new Trads springing up all the time, usually under the banner of "eclectic" Wicca: very personal ways of practicing, with bits and pieces of other Trads, the folklore of assorted cultures (usually Celtic), gods picked from here and there, and much "channeled" material. Many Wiccans, and it's impossible to say how many, prefer to practice alone as solitaries, using rituals and methods exclusively their own. It's this sort of thing that drives more traditional Trads nuts; many of them just despise these self-taught, self-initiated people, claiming that they're ruining Wicca, and calling them "Insta-Witches." I'm not going to deny that there are Insta-Witches out there, people who have read one book and decided that they know it all, but real eclectic Wiccans don't fit into that category. Eclectics are people who have studied—often studied a *lot*—on their own or perhaps in covens, and have decided that a more personal way of worshiping works best for them. As I mentioned in the chapter on deities, if it connects them to the gods, who's to say they're wrong or somehow less Wiccan than anyone else?

For all you new people, or for those of you who just want more out of your Trad or are thinking of switching, here's an oversimplified scan of the major Trads. If you want to know more, there's at least one book, and probably dozens, on each one, not to mention hordes of Web sites. I'm not going to list all those sites in the appendix: a simple Web search on the Trad names should return plenty of sites to you.

An Overview of Major Trads

Gardnerian Tradition

The root religion of Wicca. The Gardnerian Trad is initiatory, and initiates advance in the Trad through a system of three degrees, the time span between degrees no less than a year and a day. You can't just read a few books on Gardnerian Wicca and start calling yourself a Gardnerian: You have to be taught and initiated by someone who was taught and initiated by someone going all the way back to Gardner. Most of the details of the practice are oathbound: That is, you're going to have to take an oath not to reveal them. Break it, and the karmic results presumably won't be pretty, plus you can *forget* being invited to the coven Yule party. Like many subsequent Trads, Gardnerian practice invokes specific deities.

Still, enough information has leaked out about the Gardnerian practice to lend its surface structure to many other Trads: the keeping of a Book of Shadows, Drawing Down the Moon, the Great Rite, casting a Circle, calling the quarters, the use of an athame, even requiring an oath of secrecy.

Gardnerian practice came to the United States via an Englishman, Raymond Buckland, who was initiated by Gardner's high priestess, Lady Olwen, in 1964. Buckland and his wife, Rosemary, spread the word of the religion and began preparing students for initiation, keeping to the Trad's requirement of a year and a day. Buckland wrote several books, but the most influential were *Witchcraft Ancient and Modern* and *Practical Candleburning Rituals,* in 1970. This was a very opportune time, as the 1960s and 1970s were a particularly fertile ground for new ideas and practices, and people took to Wicca enthusiastically. *Buckland's Complete Book of Witchcraft,* published in 1986, is still a standard reference text for almost every new seeker, regardless of Trad. You'll hear Wiccans speaking of "Uncle Bucky's Big Blue Book"—this is the one.

If you like a free and easy, unstructured approach to Wicca, you're probably not going to be happy as a Gardnerian. They view themselves as the guardians of the sacred practices of Gardner, preserving the rituals and secrets so that they won't become tainted or die out. And they're right to do it. If they don't want to publish the details of their practice—and they swear that the full principles of belief never have been, despite several books that purport to do just that—then the only way to preserve the Trad is to make sure that the lineage is protected by one-on-one teaching.

The only drawback here is, oddly enough, that people lie about their Gardnerian lineage all the time. Some lineages are a bit shaky. And then there are those who claim a "reciprocal" initiation: They've gotten an initiation from a Gardnerian who has waived the year-and-a-day degree system, because the candidate claims to be a high priest or priestess in a similar Trad, like the Alexandrian. This definitely isn't *supposed* to happen. A real Gardnerian lineage is supposed to be your guarantee of Wiccan authenticity.

In theory, if you were considering studying with someone who claimed to be a Gardnerian, you could call the person who initiated your prospective teacher and ask. Then call the teacher's teacher, until you can verify the lineage. Sometimes, students even do this, but most want to jump right in there and take their place in the Wiccan Apostolic Succession, so they don't bother to check. Then one day they run into an authentic Gardnerian priest or priestess and find that they don't know the secret handshake, or whatever. Very embarrassing.

Another pitfall for those who would be pure and unadulterated Gardnerian is to mistake an Alexandrian for a Gardnerian. Which leads us to . . .

Alexandrian Tradition

The Alexandrians can boast of having the most famous, maybe even the first, Wiccan "grandmother" story. Alex Sanders, the founder of this Trad, claimed to have been initiated by his granny at age seven. In a 1987 documentary, *The Occult Experience,* Sanders stated that it had been a "sex initiation." She was supposed to have drawn a bit of blood by pricking his . . . well, uh, let's just say that the word *pricking* is indicative. Later, when every third Wiccan had been initiated by Granny, Sanders recanted.

He was originally initiated into a Gardnerian coven, whose members little suspected that they were nurturing a future Trad founder. And little did they suspect that one day he would publicly refer to Gardnerians as "novices."

The flamboyant Sanders was a showman on the scale of the great occultists of the occult revival. If he had been practicing in the 1880s or so, he certainly would have given Crowley, Mathers, Blavatsky, *et al.,* a run for their money. As it turned out, the 1960s, when he founded his Trad, proved a fertile time for a grandstander like Sanders. He knew perfectly how to play the press and was soon styled "King of the Witches." The publicity he generated for Wicca, and for himself, horrified the secretive Gardnerians.

The Alexandrian Tradition looked suspiciously like Gardner's. Soon there were cries of "oath breaker" ringing throughout the land. Sanders was accused of usurping Gardnerian beliefs, rituals, tools, structure, and—for all we know—the secret handshake (we don't know *for sure* that they don't have one: It's a *Mystery*).

Sanders wasn't exactly keeping the secrets. In fact, it was Sanders's aim to make Wicca more accessible: You didn't have to be initiated into the Trad in order to attend many of the Alexandrian Circles. There was and still is a degree system, however, and many Alexandrian covens are closed to outsiders. The Alexandrians are looser than the Gardnerians, with individual covens retaining their autonomy.

The most famous Alexandrians are Janet and Stewart Farrar, although Stewart recently died, leaving some excellent books. The Farrars' book, *A Witches Bible Compleat,* is the definitive work on the Alexandrian Tradition. Maybe it's best not to ask Gardnerians how they liked it.

Victor Anderson and the Faery Tradition

Faery is the Mensa of the neo-Pagan world. If you think that the word *faery* conjures up a happysweetie vision of Tinkerbell flitting among the flowers, then this Trad is definitely not for you. And if you're looking for spoon-fed Wiccan lore, you'd be advised to look elsewhere

Faery (also spelled *feri*) places heavy emphasis on personal revelatory experience, brought on by ecstatic trances and possession (which may include shape-shifting), which is the original meaning of *Mysteries*. (This is why true Mysteries can't be taught, only experienced, and no two experiences are alike.) For this reason, initiates must be thoroughly prepared, and Faery training is aimed at that purpose.

The Trad's founders, Victor and Cora Anderson, met during World War II, when both were initiates of the Harpy Coven in

Oregon. Through the years, Victor and Cora added southern folk magic, Gardnerian and Alexandrian elements, and Victor's own blend of Hawaiian Huna and Voudoun experience. In the 1970s, Anderson's most famous initiate, poet and musician Gwydion Pendderwen, added Celtic/Welsh elements, although not every Faery coven is Celtic. This association also began Faery's rich store of liturgical, mythical, and bardic material, including a Creation Myth. This is constantly growing as the Trad attracts writers, poets, artists, and musicians.

Faery is a highly personal path. For that reason, all initiates and all teachers blend their own experiences into the teaching, so that the practice remains varied. The resulting covens are very tribal in feeling, and don't lend themselves to large public gatherings. No two Faery covens will be the same, and many adherents of the Trad do solitary work. Even those who are part of a close-knit coven will find themselves doing lots of work on their own to develop the qualities necessary for the practice.

Still, there are some basics to Faery. There is no Rede or Threefold Law, but an emphasis on personal responsibility. This is definitely *not* a Trad for the neurotic or needy. They do not put up with weakness, insincerity, or self-deception, and have a strong warrior code. They work with seven deities and seven guardians, although more deities may be invoked. The group uses several exercises to strengthen the psychic energy to prepare for the revelation of the individual Mysteries.

They believe in the doctrine of the Three Selves or Souls: that all humans are made up of the Talking Self (conscience self), the God Self (energy that connects with the spiritual), and the Animal Self or Fetch, which moves energy between the Talking and God Selves.

One of the interesting elements of the Trad is the use of the inverted pentagram, called by Faery the "horned" pentagram, with one point down and two up. Most Wiccans go absolutely ballistic at the very sight of an inverted pentagram because of its use by satanists. Faery initiates ignore that whole debate as beneath them.

True Faery is complex and requires a personal commitment to preparation for the experience. This is another Trad that comprises a traceable lineage, either back to Victor and Cora Anderson or to Gwydion Pendderwen. It is not to be confused with recent shortcut versions relying on Wiccan or Celtic elements, and should not be confused with a similar-sounding version espoused by writer Kisma Stepanich.

McFarland Dianics/American Dianic Tradition

The Dianic Tradition may be the most misunderstood Trad in Wicca, especially in the United States. The common, but mistaken, belief is that all Dianic Trads exclude men and exclude male deities. This may be true for some covens or groves, but not all. The more malicious misinformation is that Dianics are man haters and lesbians, as if being a gay woman was something shameful or threatening. The gay bashing is all the more disturbing since Wicca claims to be a nonjudgmental religion.

Most Dianics include the God Consort in the appropriate rituals, and men may be initiated into some Dianic covens. But it's true that the focus of the Trad is on the female creatrix as Maiden, Mother, and Crone, the source of all life and creative energy.

The origins of Dianic Wicca came in the early 1970s, when three women, all eventually acquainted and all operating in different locations, but at about the same time period, were working within the women's movement of the late 1960s and early 1970s. These were Morgan McFarland, Z. Budapest, and Ann Forfreedom. The emphasis in the women's movement at the time was strongly political and social, but the early adherents of what would eventually become the Dianic Trads felt that political and social advancement was hollow so long as women's spirituality was being defined by religions created and directed by men, with few if any women being given voice in church doctrine, in theology, or in the pulpits.

In those Dianic covens that practice as "women only," the Tradition runs, consciously or unconsciously, back to the ancient rituals like those of the Bona Dea, the Good Goddess of the Romans, whose twice-yearly rituals were observed only by women, excluding men. Nothing male—not even the family pet—was allowed on the premises or in the vicinity, or the Mysteries would have been profaned. So well kept were the Mysteries of Bona Dea that we have only vague ideas of what they were; we know that they were presided over by the Vestal Virgins and that the purpose was to usher the Goddess into her long sleep at the Winter Mysteries, and to welcome her back at the Spring. Other women's Mysteries, like the rites of Eleusis or the ecstatic practices of the female followers of Bacchus and Dionysus, were slightly better known, but we can only speculate as to the actual rituals and practices.

The McFarland Dianics were first established in 1971 in Dallas, Texas, by Morgan McFarland and Mark Roberts, although Roberts is no longer associated with the Trad. They are now a diverse group of covens and groves, some all-female, some male and female, some gay, some straight, some mixed. They celebrate thirteen lunar Mysteries a year, with the lunar year beginning the first moon after the winter solstice. The more informal celebrations are at the equinox, solstices, and four cross-quarter days.

The Trad is initiatory, oathbound, and emphasizes the lineage. No coven exists without a high priestess who has been through initiation and a Passage Rite from another McFarland high priestess. High priests, if a particular coven chooses to work with one, are chosen by the presiding priestess. This is an honorary position with no tenure: In other words, don't believe anyone who tells you that he can initiate you into the Trad because he's an "initiated high priest." The lineage is matriarchal, and each teaching priestess holds the final decision on who is initiated. The Circles may admit guests, but coven membership is through initiation. There are no limits or rules as to the number of initiates in any coven.

McFarland Dianics maintain a Dianic Council of priestesses

who oversee the workings of the Trad. Since the Trad works from hand-copied ritual books, the Council sometimes compares the books to make sure that the integrity of the Trad rituals is maintained. At the same time, the Circles vary from coven to coven, from simple Circles to extravagant productions, so long as the basic ritual doesn't change.

The McFarland Dianics and their energetic founder are still going strong after thirty years, despite the fact that they never felt any need to "package" the Trad for widespread consumption. They held to the quaint notion that they had to know you before they'd teach you. For years, if you wanted to be a McFarland Dianic, you had to hop a plane to Dallas. Now the Trad has initiated high priestesses in several states, and, after thirty years, finally has a Web site. But it is certainly not a "learn it all from a book" Trad.

Feminist Dianics and the Susan B. Anthony Coven #1

The most famous feminist coven, the Susan B. Anthony Coven #1, was founded in San Francisco in 1971 by Zsuzsanna Budapest, known simply as "Z." When most people think of Dianic Wicca, it's the type espoused by Budapest that comes to mind: adamantly feminist, antipatriarchal, and vocally political. Budapest's vision of women's spirituality was outlined in her book *The Holy Book of Women's Mysteries*. Feminist Dianic Wicca focuses on a female-centered theology, empowering women who have decided to take back the spiritual power that was denied to them by a male-dominated religious structure. They believe that patriarchal religion has glorified war and violence, diminishing the importance of peace, happiness, and abundance, which Z. sees as female qualities. She believes that, until the time when those values come into ascendance, women should use their magical power to fight war and crime by hexing or cursing the perpetrators. Not a bad project for *both* sexes, actually.

Biology as Destiny: Some Side Notes on Feminist Wicca

Because I was so involved with the feminist movement in the 1960s and 1970s, I was appalled when I attended a women's group at a Pagan gathering a few years ago.

I thought that we had done away with the old "biology is destiny" ideas, the myth that women are limited by biological functions, and should be treated differently than men. For a long time, biology held women back: We were denied jobs because we'd just get married and pregnant, and pregnant women or mothers shouldn't work. We were thought to be more delicate than men, and incapable of many kinds of work: It was men's duty to protect us for our own good. Why give a woman a responsible job, when she was just marking time until she found a husband? Wifehood and motherhood were a woman's real fulfillment. These ingrained ideas were the most frustrating area of women's fight for equality.

Since I thought we'd done with all that, I was unprepared for what I found at the Pagan women's group twenty years later. All these women wanted to discuss was biology. That was how they defined themselves. The subjects of women's experiences were related to menstruation, childbearing, and menopause.

They devised rituals such as the ceremony in which they went off alone and bled on the ground as an offering to Mother Earth; they referred to their periods as "my moons" in an attempt to link biological function with mysticism; they were concerned about impressing upon their daughters the grave importance of first menstruation. Nothing about supporting their daughters in their first jobs, I noticed, or encouraging girls to develop their own minds and talents to be used to enrich the outside world. Thus, they drop-kicked women back to the time when we were separated from the rest of society in menstrual huts, not to be spoken to, touched, or seen. The theory for re-creating the ritual was that women are more magical during that time, and that, historically, menstruating women needed to be alone, protected by the men of ancient tribes in order to preserve their power. Never mind that there is no real proof for that assertion: It sounded more sexist than anything I'd ever heard from men.

Nothing was discussed about women's accomplishments, the contributions women have made to society, and certainly no celebration of the many women who suffered or even gave their lives in service to their country or for their convictions, including the Suffragettes, some of whom were subjected to imprisonment and mistreatment equal to anything the Inquisition came up with. There were no rituals to honor these women who formed our past. The only accomplishment the group was concerned with was childbirth. And, let's face it: Childbearing is hardly a unique accomplishment, it's a mere biological event. (Child*rearing* is the real challenge.) In this group, the primitive functions of women were elevated over our higher aspirations.

If that's what you're looking for in a feminist coven or group, good luck to you. And even more luck to your daughters.

Discordians

The original Apple Corps. If Gardnerians are the staid gatekeepers of the Wiccan religion, adhering to each and every detail as set out by Gerald B., then the Discordians are the yahoos of the Wiccan world. You know that part of the Charge of the Goddess that talks about "mirth and reverence"? The Discordians really took that "mirth" part seriously. We're not even sure they're Wiccans. Neither are they. But they show up at a lot of Wiccan and Pagan gatherings, so let's give 'em the benefit of the doubt.

Like the Gardnerians, they have specific deities, but they're not very secretive about it: They are Eris, the Greek goddess of discord and chaos; and, to a lesser extent, Loki, the Norse trickster god. Like many Wiccan groups, Discordians have an oath protecting their Mysteries. And they'll be happy to tell you what it is. *And* what the Mysteries are. Their practices are varied, to say the least. Let's just say that if you come across a group performing the Lesser Invoking Pentagram of the Velvet Elvis, or if the high priest and priestess refer to themselves as "Jake and Elwood," you can be reasonably sure you're dealing with the disciples of Eris.

They *do*, however, have a Holy Book: the *Principia Discordia,* which outlines the Mysteries as revealed by Eris to the head of the Erisian Temple P.O.E.E. (don't ask), Malaclypse the Younger, in 1954. Or maybe it was 1958. But it could have been 1969, except that there were five copies published in 1965, but they were all lost. According to the *Principia,* "We are a tribe of philosophers, theologians, magicians, scientists, artists, clowns, and similar maniacs who are intrigued with ERIS, GODDESS OF CONFUSION and with Her Doings."

Some of the more esoteric movements to come out of Discordia are the Church of the Subgenius, Bob-ism, and Salem's own Sisterhood of Thalia (the Sisters also initiate guys. Not men, *guys*—the kind who don't mind scratching private parts in public or burping during ritual).

Discordians do have a serious principle and purpose. For one thing, they remind us of the joy of life. They also believe that a mind free of dogma is a mind free. As the Holy Book says, "The human race will begin solving its problems on the day that it ceases taking itself so seriously."

Most Discordians would blush to admit to having a lineage, or Pagan origin, but they do have historical forerunners. Like the ancient shamans, many cultures had Holy Fools who were insane—or acted irrationally—and were thought to have been struck mad by the gods, who then used the Fools as their instruments.

Is Discordia for everyone? Maybe not, but *definitely* not if you like your hot dogs with buns. If you like apples, though, especially of the golden variety, you're home free. Hail, Eris.

Hereditary/Family Witchcraft

Not Wicca, but interesting in its own right. This is an area that is so difficult to prove or disprove that an entire body of faulty folklore has sprung up around it. Three out of ten Witches you meet claim to have learned or inherited their powers from Granny, who got the whole shebang from an unbroken line back to the Stone Age, which they insist makes them more psychic than thou.

I'm not saying that hereditary Witches don't exist, I'm just saying that they're probably much rarer than the numbers of people who claim to be hereditary Witches would suggest. One feature of hereditary Witchcraft is supposed to be the secrecy surrounding it: Witches claiming inherited practices say that the reason their families never said anything was for fear of persecution. That's strange, since there were many periods of time, usually around the end of a century, when occultism was so much in vogue that there would have been very little danger of persecution. And if it's supposed to be kept secret, why talk about it now? Another is that many people claiming it say their family practices have survived from Pagan times; others say they are *unchanged* since Pagan times, which is even more doubtful, because nothing survives for that long without some mutation. The real giveaway is when the "ancient family practices" include things that are obviously modern Wiccan, like the Rede or Masonic ritual.

Authentic family or hereditary witches usually *aren't* talking about it, much less running around Pagan gatherings touting their "lineages." Why should they? If the family Trads have survived this long without publicity, they aren't about to change it. And recruitment just isn't something they do: Either you're born into it, or you marry into it. Numbers are the last thing on their minds. They're certainly not interested in teaching every potential Witch who wants to start casting money spells.

One of the most amusing accounts of "Hereditary Traditional Family Witchcraft" was found on a Web site purporting to come from a woman who is, she claimed, one of "the Few." According to this, there are six families in Ireland who are "true examples" of these old ways, practices that have survived since Pagan times. The site then goes on to list a mishmash of bloodlines, select members of the family who are singled out to learn the secrets (many times with the rest of the family being unaware they have an exalted magician in their midst), and detail how the secrets are passed on to the selected women (*of course,* these powerful secrets are for women only). For the occasional unfortunate family member who somehow fails to be initiated into Granny's secrets, or just can't make sense out of the family Grimoire (*naturally,* there's a Grimoire), there awaits a grisly future: She's doomed to wander restlessly her entire life, feeling incomplete and unfulfilled, directionless, with no outlet for her awesome powers. I got the feeling that she'd eventually end up as a character on *All My Children.*

If this all sounds familiar to you, you've probably read Anne Rice's Mayfair Witches series. It's a pretty good bet that the author of this site has it memorized, and is probably keeping an eagle eye out for the Talamasca lurking in every corner.

This particular site, whose language swells with melodramatic phrases as the author's indignation rises, goes on to cite the usual erroneous information that the Burning Times was actually persecution by the new cabal of Evil Male Doctors to rid themselves of female midwives and herbalists. And the author ends by dramatically beating her brow over the rising tide of jealous and enraged Wiccans who resent "the Few's" enormous power and ancient secrets. She blames Wicca for the "dwindling numbers" of those hereditary Witches, the real, true, honest-ta-Gawd practitioners. I don't understand this part: They're supposed to be family Witches, so why don't they just stay home and breed? That's generally a cure for dwindling numbers. And it would give them something to do besides read Anne Rice.

And what has caused this gross indignity? Wicca and the Internet! Yes, friends, the proliferation of Wiccans discussing their religion on the Internet and in public has endangered the Great Irish Witch Families. Apparently, all we motor-mouth Wiccans—especially of the American and Australian variety—have been making the religion waaaaay too public, and people have gotten the idea that Wicca is the only form of Witchcraft. Those same upstarts sometimes claim that *they're* hereditary or traditionals, too; what an outrage. And to add insult to injury, Wiccans have the gall to try to have Wicca recognized as a real world religion, with the "Mysteries being accessible to all." This is just terrible for the hereditary traditional Witches because . . . well, okay, frankly, I can't understand why it's so terrible for them. They're supposed to be keeping these great secrets and practicing the One True Real Witchcraft (which isn't Wicca), no one is supposed to know who they are, and they're not supposed to volunteer any information, especially to us plebeians. So why should they give a shite (Irish, ya know) if Wicca's getting all this attention? *They're* not supposed to want any. As the writer put it—unintentionally hilariously— ". . . ignorant acolytes of Wicca run amok through the once secluded glade of Hecate." (Although, last time I checked, Hecate was a Greco-Roman goddess. I guess the Great Irish Witch Families have never heard of Brigit or Macha or the Morrigan.)

At that point, I'm afraid I spewed my mouthful of Phony American Wiccan Mead all over my keyboard.

And they say Witches have no sense of humor! I'm hoping that the site was an elaborate joke, but I have my doubts.

Choosing a Trad or Coven

You'll notice that many of these Trads have training programs and degree systems. While many have occasional open Circles where anyone may attend, most do their serious magical work only with those who have been initiated and understand the way they work and what the coven hopes to accomplish. Unless everyone is working together under a similar system, magical workings aren't as effective, if they work at all. Also, when doing serious magic, there is a strong element of trust that is absolutely necessary: People who have trained and worked together get to know the limits and strengths of each other's energy, which comprise the limits and strength of the entire coven.

Individuality is important in some Trads, so that the diversity can be used for the good of the whole coven. One person may be an herbalist, one may be a gifted reader, one a healer or a natural teacher, and so on.

If you're considering joining or changing Trads, you need to assess your own needs first and identify exactly what you're looking for, spiritually. And don't just choose on the basis of how "magical" or "exclusive" a Trad seems. Also look at the training and exactly what they're teaching: Is the training aimed simply at keeping out the undesirables, or is it aimed, like Faery, at preparing the individual for the personal and transformative Mysteries that should be ongoing in authentic spirituality? If you're asked to contribute your energy, you should know clearly what you're contributing it *to:* How and by whom is your karmic contribution being used?

Whatever Trad or coven you choose, you can't expect it to be perfect. This is one of the things that leads to so much disappointment and resulting bitterness: Coven leaders and members turn out to be only human. Some newcomers have the unreal expectation that the coven or the priestess or priest will take responsibility for you, provide the nurturing hand-holding that you didn't get from your last religion or your family or your ex-sweetie, be all-knowing and all-forgiving, and change your life without your having to lift a finger. While covens are supportive of their members, they can't solve your problems for you. The coven is not your therapist. You're expected to keep learning, to grow up, to do your part, not just show up and vent every week.

A coven or a Trad consists of people who have come together to do a specific work, either purely spiritual, purely magical, or a combination. If you're a beginner, it's the coven's job to train you so that you become an equal and take your responsible place in the Circle, making an equal contribution. You are expected to do the work and take some initiative. And don't assume that the coven has to take you, even if you want to join. They don't. *You* may not be right for *them.* The personal chemistry may be off.

If you're changing Trads or covens, don't assume that because you're a high mucky-muck with degrees in another Trad, it makes you special and exempt from the training program. In fact, you may be required to start over. And something nobody needs to hear is: "Well, in Lady Moira Celticthanthou's coven, where I was an Initiated and Elevated Tenth Degree, *we* did it *this* way." If it was so great, why aren't you still there? It looks suspiciously like you may have been booted out. At the very least it establishes you as a Third Degree Pain in the Ass.

7

The Image of Wicca

There's a lot of talk among Wiccans as to the image we project to the rest of the world. We're very concerned that people should take us seriously as a religion. And that's a valid concern.

But before we can convince anyone else, we need to understand what we're saying and the best way to say it. We need to get more selective about the interviews we give and in what setting we give them, and about the image that we ourselves are projecting.

"Dispelling the myths of Witchcraft," "correcting misinformation" and "banishing the stereotype of Witches," are catchphrases that come up almost constantly. Go to almost any Wiccan Web site, or talk to almost any Witch, and you'll hear people parroting the same ideas, in almost the same language. It's as if they memorized a list. And in a way, they did: These Web sites and Wiccan books seem to pick up the same ideas in the same words from each other, like a virus. Perhaps it's just because we've been having to say the same things over and over: No, we don't worship the Devil; No, male Witches aren't called warlocks; No, we don't perform blood sacrifices; ad infinitum. You get to the point where you almost say them in your sleep. I've got to hand it to longtime public Wiccans like Starhawk, Margot Adler, Selena Fox, Marion Weinstein, and others: The ability to answer the same dumb questions over and over, still smiling, after all this time, and not punch somebody out, has got to be a gift from the gods.

But we might ask ourselves why we're having to repeat the same information when dealing with people outside Wicca. After all, Wicca is now very trendy. Documentary-type TV shows, such as programs on the Discovery Channel and the Travel Channel, have done excellent segments on Wicca. Joan Rivers once devoted an entire show to Wicca, inviting four practicing Wiccans to give their views. Even Oprah had a show on Wicca, although she made the mistake of also inviting two loudmouthed evangelical fundamentalists who managed to embarrass Christians everywhere. And even small-town newspapers and TV news shows are hot to interview the local Witches at Halloween.

With all the media exposure, why are we having to explain ourselves and our religion so often?

Many Witches don't like the images of Wicca presented by TV shows. But you have to give most producers credit for trying to be fair, especially producers of the documentaries. In the majority of cases, they weren't misrepresenting anyone: They went looking for Wiccans and could only present what they found. If they're getting mixed messages from us—if how we *act* differs from what we *say*—how can they tell the difference? And the image that we create is the one we have to live with.

It's time that we took a hard look at the images that we ourselves are presenting to the media and to the rest of the world. We consistently refer to Wicca as "the Craft" instead of as a religion. Wiccans used to refer to Wicca as "the Old Religion," which wasn't accurate either, but at least reinforced the idea of religion. We repeat phrases from books, some of them incomprehensibly out of context. Some of them are incomprehensible even *within* the context. As an example, many Salem Witches parrot Laurie Cabot's phrase, "People were hanged under the wrong definition of Witchcraft," but fail to expand on what that definition was (diabolism, if you're interested). Another Cabot phrase, this to explain why Witches wear black, is about black being "the culmination of all vibrational light on the material plane." Ex-*cuse* me? *What?* And also . . . *so* what? Without explanation, the phrases mean nothing to the average non-Wiccan layperson. Sometimes they mean very little to the average Witch. And yet Wiccans repeat the phrases, or variations, without really thinking about them or explaining what they mean. After talking to many Witches who repeat this particular phrase, I'm convinced that they have no idea what it *does* mean. Cabot is talking about black drawing in light, and light being the carrier of vibrations and, therefore, energy. While her explanation is logical in the context of her own teaching of "Witchcraft as a Science," it does nothing to answer the simple question about why Witches wear black, unless she goes into the long version. And that does not translate well into a sound bite. (Also, many Witches disagree with her physics, saying that black is the *absence* of light, while white is the presence of the entire spectrum.)

There's no denying that we're sometimes forced to take a defensive position when asked questions that are basically silly. You wonder how educated people—which is what the media are supposed to be—can really ask questions about Witches flying on brooms and turning people into toads. Yet when they ask, we give them some long and very dubious quasi-historical folderol about supposed Pagan customs having to do with brooms and flying ointment (both of which became associated with witches during the witch hysteria) instead of just saying, "Uh, people can't fly on brooms. Look up. Have you ever *seen* anyone flying on a broom?" Questions like these are obviously frivolous, and they don't deserve serious answers. They deserve to be dismissed so that we can get on to more serious subjects.

But we have to take ourselves to task for feeding into that silliness. In the first place, we need to make sure that we've got our facts from reliable sources, not from the latest Insta-Witch book. We need to read outside the confining context of Wicca, branching into the larger arenas of history, folklore, anthropology, and religion. Instead of rattling off some mystical-sounding gobbledegook, we need to give straightforward answers to specific questions, rather than trying to supply the entire history of witchcraft and magic according to the latest pop historian.

Until we begin to act with dignity, we can't possibly be taken seriously. By *dignity* and *seriously,* I don't mean "humorless." In fact, part of our problem is that we come across as *so* humorless, *so* joyless, *so* ready to be offended. And this in a religion that says it's concerned with the celebration of nature and the joy of life. If you go along with Doreen Valiente's Charge of the Goddess, note that it mentions having both mirth and reverence within you. We're very short on the "mirth" part, and there's some equivocation about the "reverence." How can you revere the gods while wearing silly fang teeth in the Circle? Even worse, what are you really saying about Wicca as a serious religion while you're dressed in an unusual costume and spouting incomplete rote phrases, or babbling on about your "psychic powers?"

The Parade of the Undertakers

You want joyless? Let me tell you about a local parade in Salem.

Almost every city or town has a founders' day parade that takes place on the anniversary of the founding of the town. In Salem it's called "Heritage Day," and the parade is a big deal: Practically every organization in town marches in it.

Anyway, this particular Heritage Day, I had some health problems and was watching the goings-on instead of participating. It was a terrific day for a parade: sunny, warm weather, lots of cheerful crowds. The Shriners (who are Masons of the advanced degrees and do a lot of community work, and whose burn hospitals for children are famous) represented about a third of the parade, with marching bands, Dixieland bands, grown men in funny hats on motor scooters, and clowns working the crowd and collecting for the hospitals. The fire department had dalmatians riding on the fire trucks. After them came a large group of young people, all in white, metallic gold, and turquoise, waving golden banners, clapping, dancing, singing upbeat songs. This was the youth group of a local church, and they looked like they were enjoying every minute. Then came our local politicians, many with supporters handing out candy and cracking jokes. There were Highland Pipers looking and sounding good. The entire parade was movement, color, and laughter.

And then came a wave of darkness that looked for all the world like the Associated Funeral Directors of Salem and the Surrounding Counties. They were all in black, apparently the result of some sort of demented dress code. Some were wearing heavy-looking capes—at noon, in *August*. A couple wheeled baby carriages—at noon, in August—to show that we're Just Like Anyone Else. Anyone who subjects a little baby to the relentless sun throughout a fairly long march, that is. Most didn't smile or work the crowd. They didn't wave. They carried banners, but most of those were black too, or somber purple. They sang, sort of. What they were singing, "We All Come From the Goddess," was sung slow enough to be a dirge. The accompanying drums kept the same solemn beat. There was, at least, a pickup truck with a threesome playing an electric piano and smacking tambourines, but you couldn't hear them. Occasionally there was a confrontational chant of "Never Again!"

The Witches had arrived, and with them a heavy load of Serious Religion.

The entire marching unit seemed to cast a pall over the crowd. The laughing died down, everyone stared with an uncomfortable stillness. It was as if the sun had gone behind a cloud. Or the Puritans were back in town.

When they had marched on, the parade gaiety resumed.

And I thought, *What was* that *all about? What are we* doing?" If the Witches' contingent was supposed to be showing that our religion was one of nature and light and spiritual joy, they sure failed, big-time. Being from New Orleans, I've seen jollier parades at funerals. Frankly, the Christian youth group did a lot better at projecting the joys of religion. I'm all for taking religion seriously, but in a summer parade? I'd never realized how inappropriate it was.

So. What's the deal? Witches and Wiccans spend a lot of time moaning about the misinterpretation of our religion and the persistence of stereotypes of the Witch—and here they were, Wicked Queen look-alikes, reinforcing just about every stereotype anyone ever held about us.

Salem witches have always had an "us versus them" attitude anyway with regard to the larger community, an attitude long unquestioned by most Witches, who never made any real attempt to join in the community at large, except as retail merchants. There's been much moaning about Witches never being invited to join civic committees, but how many of us actually worked up the initiative to *ask* to join? It was as if the modern Witches had already determined that the town was the same as it was in 1692: out to get 'em. They overlook the fact that Witches are Salem residents too, and entitled to join in community efforts, from politics to local charities and public projects. But when the Witches did join in, as in the Heritage Day parade, they were determined to do it with chips on their shoulders and on their own stiff-backed terms. The participation in the Heritage Day parade began in 1992, the three hundredth anniversary of the witch trials, as a protest. Then it was billed as a "reminder that Witches would never be oppressed again," a valid enough sentiment. But believe me, the people of Salem do not need to be reminded: They *know*. They are descendants of persecutors and persecuted alike, now living in the same community and working together. They're not really interested in oppressing anybody. Another point of the Witches marching is supposedly to show that "we're here to stay!" Well, okay, but who asked us to go? Maybe some local rabid fundamentalists don't like Witches, but they don't like the Catholics or Jews, either.

And why did the Witches assume that they needed to make this point in an adversarial manner? Why didn't they assume that they could march in the parade simply because they're part of Salem like any other church group, singing happy songs and making an effort to show they're part of the community? Why didn't they dress like everyone else, if they wanted to show that they're no different from everyone else? Or, since this was summer, if they wanted to swelter in robes, how about some solar colors of red, gold, orange? The summer Sabbats are supposed to be joyous times, so why the solemn gloom of Samhain?

In Salem, there are a couple of simple answers: *Because it looks good on the evening news.* And the answer from one of the organizers: *So everyone will know how many Witches are in Salem.* I can assure you, the number of Witches marching in the parade is in no way indicative of the number of Witches in Salem. Many Witches here don't feel the need to take to the streets in order to show that their religion is valid.

Of course, Salem is different from any other town because there is a higher concentration of Witches here. It's hard to be exact: I'm guessing perhaps five hundred practicing Witches in a town of thirty-eight thousand people, based on the number that show up for various events, and taking into account the solitaries and the Witches who want nothing to do with public events. This is despite some local Witches' ludicrous declaration that there are two or three thousand. Even accepting those numbers, though, you'd think that the Witches could accomplish a lot as a voting bloc or an organized political committee—but past attempts to get Witches to register to vote haven't been very successful. Aside from an abortive, publicity-propelled candidacy for mayor a few years back, no such thing has happened. A few Witches do serve on the committee for Haunted Happenings, the town's annual monthlong Halloween festival, but they're there as merchants, to promote their Witch-related businesses. In this town, it's pretty much all about money.

An Alternative View of the Green-Faced Witch

Around Halloween, you'll find Wiccans up in arms about the traditional Halloween image of Witches as ugly, misshapen old women with green faces. Many Witches actively look for examples of this image, so they can complain in loud voices about how insulting it is.

But let's consider where that image may have originated.

In the first place, Witches didn't turn green until *The Wizard of Oz*. Wicked Witches, anyway—you'll notice that Glinda the Good Witch wasn't green. Who knows why the makeup designers decided that the Wicked Witch of the West should have a green face? Maybe it was because of her envy of Glinda: you know, "green with envy"? We can be pretty sure it wasn't because she was equated with the Green Man.

The Wizard of Oz was so popular that makers of Halloween decorations adopted the green face for the image of the wicked Witch. Speaking of popularity, some of the most vocal of the anti-green face group profess to be great admirers of *The Wizard of Oz*, especially the Witch of the West. So how upset could they really be?

Many Witches moan and groan about the green-faced image, without even considering why it's insulting. They'll equate it with illustrations of hook-nosed Jews and watermelon-eating African Americans. Not a fair comparison: Those two images were deliberately designed and published to provoke hate and distrust (the Jewish illustrations) and ridicule (the "lazy Negro" lounging around eating watermelon while everyone else works) toward specific groups. Those images arose out of social conditions of fear and stupidity.

The green-faced Witch arose from a movie makeup decision. The image was never intended to provoke hate or prejudice against Witches or Wiccans—it's a pretty fair guess that whoever designed the green makeup had no idea that real Witches even existed. And most people who dress up as Witches at Halloween and paint their faces green, or who manufacture Halloween decorations, do *not* do it in order to deliberately insult anybody.

This isn't to say that people shouldn't be made aware that we'd rather not be portrayed as wicked or ugly, but we should do a more sensitive and informed job of telling them about it.

The Pagan poet Angel once wrote a beautiful piece titled "The Halloween Witch" that gave us a whole new way of thinking about this image. I'm not saying that this is actually where the image came from (it most likely is not), and neither is Angel, but it does give us pause.

Consider, Angel says, that people accused of witchcraft disappeared from their homes, taken away in the middle of the night and thrown into jails. They weren't seen again for months. In jail, they were tortured until they confessed and then were presented to the public, after unrelenting abuse, as confessed witches. By that time, they probably *did* have green faces: swollen and covered with fresh and healing bruises. Their noses had been broken, teeth knocked out, hanks of hair and scalp torn off, fingers broken with the nails ripped away, broken or dislocated arms and legs, unable to stand up straight. A formerly normal-looking woman was transformed into a terrifying hag for public edification—because she was a confessed witch.

Angel goes on to suggest that the next time we see a green-faced Halloween Witch, we revere her courage and remember her as a symbol of those who died.

More harmful to the image of Witches is the *reaction* of Wiccans when confronted with a green-faced image. We've been dealing with this image for years, and most of us are resigned to it by now and long ago ceased to feel any real insult. We simply sigh and explain patiently. But instead of explaining, all too many Wiccans immediately get on a high horse, expressing an indignation that they may not even feel, but think that they *should* feel.

This knee-jerk reaction can be carried to ridiculous extremes. As an example, this past Samhain some Witches set up a "Magickal

Arts Center" here in Salem. This was great, because we could use a community center. Part of the purpose of the center was to explain to tourists what Wicca is and isn't, to give a positive image of the religion. All well and good. Until four tourist women showed up at the door. These ladies had been to the face-painting booth at the street fair and had gotten the deluxe job—paint, glitter, the works. One of them had been painted and glittered green.

Now, how was she supposed to know what that meant? She wasn't a Wiccan, she was just the usual Halloween tourist, one of the estimated forty thousand who come here during October. And she and her friends were curious about Wicca, which is why they came to the center, which advertised itself as giving out information on the subject. This was supposed to be the logical place to find out what Wicca is.

They were treated very rudely. The Wiccan at the door took one look and immediately became indignant, telling the green one, "Your friends can come in, but you can't." The tourist lady didn't have a clue. "Why not me?" she said.

The door-Witch went on about how insulting the woman's makeup was, in tones that implied that the woman had done it on purpose. She told the woman that she wouldn't be allowed in until she got rid of the makeup. Now, in a town where you're hard-pressed to find so much as a Porta-Potty at this time of year, where was she going to find a place to wash her face?

Very embarrassed, the woman and her friends left.

But this poor lady was really on a roll of bad luck. She and her friends left the center and went next to the store of a local Big Name Pagan, to buy some books and get them signed. Not only were they not allowed in there either, the woman was booed and ridiculed.

Behavior like this is much more damaging to Wiccans than is any green-faced Halloween decoration. The worst part is that I'm sure the Wiccans felt very self-righteous about it all, that they were "correcting misinformation" about Witches.

Unfortunately, they managed to create just one more image of Wicca: that we're all rude.

I know that it's sometimes hard to be patient when you're being asked the same old questions, but come on: Give non-Wiccans credit for being interested enough to ask, especially if they're being polite. Show some class, people.

Professional Witches

When Wicca becomes tied to money, you're on very slippery ground. Because we're a tourist town, we see a lot of this in Salem, but it happens everywhere.

Many Witches promote themselves to raise the cost of readings: Here in my town, some Witches charge up to $150 for a half-hour reading when the norm is around $20 or $25. Worse are the people claiming to be Witches or Wiccans when they're really fortune-tellers who are using Wicca in order to make a buck: It gives them a more mysterious aura that really thrills the suckers. They make a lot of noise and publicity trying to become well-known, since the cost of their readings rises accordingly.

In Salem, many October Circles and Wiccan events are tied to stores or to tourist attractions. This past Halloween, there was the "Authentic Witch's Spell-Working Performed by Practicing Witches of Salem" under the auspices of a haunted-house-type tourist attraction. Here, you could attend an "Authentic Witches' Circle" and have a spell worked for you—at six dollars a pop. If it had been a fake Circle it would almost have been better, but unfortunately it was a Circle cast by an employee of the tourist trap, a woman claiming to be a real high priestess with degrees in several Traditions.

Since the tourist place is next door to the tiny outdoor memorial park for the 1692 trial victims, the same attraction uses the memorial grounds to sponsor a "Midnight Witches' Circle." If you've ever been in Salem for Halloween, you'll know that it bears a marked resemblance to New Orleans's Bourbon Street at Mardi

Gras: The streets are crowded with drunks after about 9 P.M. So, there's a "Midnight Witches' Circle" held outdoors (on the grounds of the memorial to the 1692 victims, no less) in the glare of bare lightbulbs strung all over the grounds of a tacky tourist trap, with spooky sounds and music blaring from loudspeakers (the same loudspeakers that had all day been blaring "See the Witches' Circle at midnight!"), with a lit-up sausage-vendor cart not five feet away, and two or three carnival-style trailers selling fried dough and cider about ten feet on the other side. Plus the drunks standing around making wisecracks and laughing. Not exactly many Wiccans' idea of sacred space. Not to mention the damage to the memorial done by the especially unsavory behavior of people trampling the grass, standing on the stone walls, and dropping garbage.

But the priest and priestess of the organization that conducts the Circles maintain that they're raising awareness of Wicca because they also hand out pamphlets about Witchcraft. And personally, I think that they honestly believe they are. They've failed to see that they're merely moneymaking props for yet another tourist trap, publicly associating Wicca with unmitigated sleaze.

If you come to Salem in October, come for Halloween to have fun, *not* to celebrate the religious holy time of Samhain. Frankly, you'd be better off doing a meaningful ritual at home or, if you're a tourist, in your hotel room, *then* going out to party. There are a few public Circles, one or two of them huge, and a couple that you have to pay to attend, but do you really want this kind of impersonal, by-the-numbers ritual with strangers—some of them way *beyond* strange!—on one of the religion's most sacred days?

It's probably time to emphasize the difference between Halloween and Samhain. If you're Wiccan, you know what Samhain represents.

But Halloween is not a holy day for Pagans. If anything, it's a Christian holiday, the night before All Soul's or All Saint's Day, which is definitely not part of our religious calendar. When Wiccans celebrate Halloween, it should be for fun: for the Halloween parties, trick-or-treating (any holiday that involves free candy is a good holiday), monsters, ghosts, and all manner of spooky stuff.

We should keep trying very hard to disconnect Halloween from Samhain, to make clear the distinction in the minds of the public. This is possibly the worst time of the year for us to be so visible, but nobody ever comes looking for a Witch on May Day.

Connecting Wiccans and Witches to the European witch hysteria and to the Salem witch trials is fraught with peril. In the first place, you're connecting yourself to a definition of witchcraft that includes diabolism. Witchcraft in that period meant someone who was in league with the Devil, who placed curses and existed to do evil deeds. In the second place, if you were accused of being a witch, it meant you were accused of heresy or diabolism. It certainly did not mean that you were charged with calling the Element of Water in an Alexandrian extravaganza.

Wiccans, especially, have a very tenuous link with the Salem trials, since nobody who was accused or executed was an actual Witch in any sense of the word. Look into the records of the trials or the literature written by Robert Calaf and others directly after the trials and you'll see no references to Wicca, the Threefold Law, the Wiccan Rede, or anything else that constitutes Wiccan practice. What you *will* see is a connection of the accused to the Devil. Frankly, the modern Satanists have more grounds for indignation than we have.

So it's fairly disturbing to see Wiccans attempting to connect modern Wicca to the deaths of Christian victims, especially when it's done for money.

There are a lot of Witch stores in Salem, which is no problem. People need and want to buy things: wands, incense, herbs, crystals, candles, books. (I'm all for buying *books!*) Many Wiccan or Pagan stores, especially in smaller towns, are the hub of Pagan life in their areas. You're entitled to run a business and make a living, and you shouldn't have to use history to justify yourself.

Connecting commerce to presecution is just ludicrous. One

store and its employees took great offense at a local haunted house tourist attraction, saying that it commercialized Witchcraft. Naturally, they had to call up the press in order to make their views perfectly clear.

When the reporter looked around the Witch shop, which contained some pricey merchandise, she asked how this store was any less commercial, or taking less advantage of the Salem witch trials than a haunted house. Seemed a logical question.

But the owner was adamant that it was different. ". . . My business is a polarization of what happened here three hundred years ago. . . . It's strictly a retail business, here to educate and help heal the earth."* Followed by the usual rant about the Salem trials.

The question is what a retail business does to heal the earth. Especially any retail business carrying goods manufactured under dubious conditions in Taiwan. You're in business. You need to make a living. Everyone should understand that. Why so defensive? And what's with the "polarization" stuff? To paraphrase from Mel Brooks's *Blazing Saddles,* it's authentic Salem-witch gibberish. The lady wanted publicity for her store, and she and her employees created a bogus controversy to get it, using the Salem trials as a pretext.

This technique is certainly not limited to Salem, because I've seen and heard about similar happenings in other communities. Listen, it's no accident that these "controversies" tend to come around Halloween, or when the latest Hollywood movie about Witches is about to be released. The press is looking for a good story, the Witches are glad to garner the publicity for the business. But exploiting the deaths of innocent people is a deplorable way to get it.

When you're talking about Witchcraft and money, we Wiccan writers aren't doing it for free, either. We collect advances for our books and fees for public speaking. Some Wiccan writers make a

*From *North Shore Sunday,* October 1, 1995, by Heather Anderson.

living this way, just like writers of novels or regular nonfiction books and articles. But jeeze . . . at least admit it. Nothing makes me madder than a Wiccan writer pontificating about how his or her book was done In Service to the Goddess, without a thought to fame or fortune. Yeahrightsure. It's too hard and takes too much out of your life to write an entire book of a few hundred pages unless you have a hope of being paid. When you write a book, you really *do* want it to change somebody's life or do some good in the world or just satisfy someone's need for information. When you get a letter from a reader saying that it made a difference to him or her, you treasure it. Writers live for that stuff. And no writer can deny the ego factor: You want to say something and you want to be read.

But if we didn't want to be paid, we'd be saying what we have to say by putting it on the Internet, so people can read it at no charge and without being nagged for money to defray costs of the site.

Speaking of Web sites, it's just my little whim, but if you're putting up a site that consists mainly of your own opinions, and you've archived them back to the Stone Age so that no one should miss a single golden word of infinite wisdom, then you should bear the cost because . . . you know . . . who asked ya?

But if people are using your site beyond that, if you're loading it with useful information that takes up a lot more bandwidth than your opinion pages, if people are flocking to your site and you've got to pay for all that traffic, and if you're keeping the site updated regularly (a horrendous, time-consuming job), then you deserve to ask for some support. Especially if you're not subjecting viewers to ads. Even if you are, those ads usually don't cover the costs.

Neopagan.com, Witches' Voice, Circle Sanctuary, Circle of Souls Radio (a really fun site! News and Pagan music!), the Covenant of the Goddess, the Pagan Federation, in the United Kingdom, and other useful sites come immediately to mind. (More sites plus URLs in the appendix pages.) Not all these sites are asking for money, but come on . . . you know they're expensive to run. If you're using them a lot, kick in a few bucks or join the organizations they represent, which help pay the bills. Do you really need one more quartz crystal? Give the money to your favorite Web site.

Becoming the Media's Bitch

There's a reason why media people converge on Salem every Halloween. They don't want to talk to the Witches back home, who dress like everyone else and go into the office every morning: They want to talk to someone who'll dress up like their idea of what a Witch looks like and who won't mind posing in a graveyard for the interview. Salem's full of Witches who'll do anything media people ask them, and the most dangerous place on earth is between a Salem Witch and a camera. Why these Witches agree to roam through graveyards for the media is a mystery to me: What do graveyards, which are not part of our religion, have to do with Wicca?

Media folks have filmed many Wiccan Circles here, but the most outrageous was one on—surprise!—Halloween at Gallows Hill. This was supposed to be a legitimate Samhain Circle, but it was merely Halloween. They had scaffolding for the cameras, sound trucks, and huge fog machines pumping out fake fog through enormous tubes in such quantities that people were coughing and choking. The lights were blinding. A busload of tourists joined in, all carrying lit candles. The Wiccan organizers of this media event actually attempted to carry on a Circle, which many people felt was an offense both to the gods and to the spirits, not to mention rather demeaning to the people standing in the Circle. How are you supposed to honor your ancestors and the spirits of the dead when the rites keep stopping and starting in order to improve the camera angles? The funniest part was that the presiding high priestess didn't deign to join the festivities until all the cameras and lights were ready; then she proceeded to make the grand entrance, like a petulant movie star alighting from her trailer on the set. You could almost hear, "I'm ready for my close-up now, Mr. De Mille."

Okay, it was kind of a hoot to many of us observers, who had originally come there expecting an actual Circle, but what did it say about Wicca? Some friends and I were standing on the outskirts with a Druid priest from out of town whose jaw was hanging open in shock. He was the *second* funniest thing about it: He just couldn't get over the goings-on. He kept saying, "What has this circus got to do with Samhain?" "Welcome to Salem," we told him.

Little did I know that the fog machine was merely part of a trend. I've heard from at least two covens in different cities who have used them. This is strange from a religion that's supposed to revere nature: using a machine to generate *fake* nature. The ultimate in Urban Pagan Hip. The wackiest part of this is that the Salem priestess had previously and publicly claimed to be able to control the weather. I guess the God of Fog had another gig that night.

This annual Gallows Hill Walk from the site of the hangings to the witch trial memorial is a rather strange thing for Wiccans to do anyway. It was first organized in 1992 when the media descended on Salem at the three hundredth anniversary of the trials. The key word here is *media*. Alerted by the ever-present press releases, the cameras, lights, and microphones followed the crowd all the way.

At that time, and ever since, the walk is supposed to be about "remembering the victims." How come nobody bothers to remember the victims at any other time of year, when the tourists aren't around? The last of the Salem hangings occurred on the autumn equinox, putting an end to the deaths. How come no one honors the victims at Mabon, when it would be more appropriate? Because there are more tourist dollars around at Halloween?

And once again, what do those victims, pitiful and tragic as they are, have to do with us? Wiccans in Salem are constantly screaming about not being associated with diabolism, but that's exactly what the Salem victims were accused of: consorting with the Devil.

Something's really wrong here.

If you're an out-of-the-closet Wiccan and you're doing a lot of interviews, or you're connected with a prominent Wiccan/Pagan publication or coven or Web site, or you're a Wiccan writer, you might be asked to advise on a movie, TV show, or other project, or to endorse one. Please be careful about this, because you can really get screwed. The entertainment industry, especially, is an old hand at shafting you so smoothly and so quickly that you'll never realize you've been bonked and not kissed until it's all over.

Three Wiccans who should have known better fell into this trap. They were asked to preview a movie that was horrendously insulting to Wicca. The moviemakers had a pretty good idea of what the reaction would be among serious Wiccans, so they had planned a preemptive strike. The preview was intended to produce a good review, a virtual endorsement of the movie by a respected Wiccan Web site and by representatives of the Salem community. Hollywood does what it does best: It put the trio on a plane, booked them into a nice hotel, wined and dined them, made them feel like they were insiders, fed them flattery with a forklift, and gave them special trinkets connected with the movie. They were so dazzled to be part of the limelight that they gushed on about the fabulous experience and about the movie like it was *Citizen Kane*. Which it most certainly was not.

If you're asked to consult on a media project, all you can do is your best. You can talk your little heart out about the religion of Wicca and what we believe and how we practice, but when it comes down to writing an actual script, the screenwriters and directors are going to go with what sells tickets. And that's usually the most sensationalized aspects of Witchcraft. More than one Witch has sat through a horrifying film that did Wicca more harm than good, only to cringe at his or her name at the end of the credits as "consultant."

I know whereof I speak on this subject. There's an interview on the Travel Channel that I'd give my eyeteeth to do over again, because this time, I'd dress like a human being and not like Morticia Addams. At no other time do I dress in black robes: They stayed in the closet until the cameras started turning. Talk about being the media's bitch! I knew that the only way they'd talk to me was if I was dressed according to their expectations. Looking back, I should have insisted on wearing regular clothes and told them exactly *why* I was insisting: because you're supposed to be asking me about my religion, which has zilch to do with my wardrobe.

I was also asked to consult on a movie, which was supposed to star—get this—*Sylvester Stallone* in a Witch-related thriller set in Salem. This screenwriter had to have been joking. The project fell through, and it was probably a good thing that it did.

I finally wised up. Recently I did an interview in regular clothes, and the British interviewer started the questions with "Why aren't you dressed like a Witch?" I replied that I *was* dressed like a Witch, *exactly* like one, and why wasn't he dressed like an Englishman, with the umbrella and the bowler hat? I told him that you can't tell what religion a person is just by the way he or she is dressed. Unless you're talking to the pope. Can't mistake that hat. In a couple of sentences, we were away from Halloween stereotypes and back into religion, which is exactly where we should have been in the first place.

Witches rationalize some pretty strange behavior by saying that whatever you have to do to get the media's attention is okay; that once you have it, you can tell the real truth about Wicca. Just remember that actions speak louder than words. Don't insist on the dignity of your religion when you look like you're on your way to a Goth rave and you're traipsing around a graveyard with a candle under your face, waving a crystal wand and intoning a spell.

To draw a parallel: For years, the famous Dr. Kevorkian had some worthwhile things to say about the issues of euthanasia and the individual's control over his or her own quality of life when the end of it was imminent. Agree with him or not, he was still taken seriously and invited to discuss his views in dignified forums. When he started daring the police to arrest him, sending a TV show a film of him helping someone to die, dressing like Uncle Sam and raving at his trial, he was dismissed as just another loony. His arguments for euthanasia were as valid as they had always been, but nobody was listening. He'd lost sight of his ultimate goal, which was supposed to be the right of the individual to terminate his or her own life in the face of horrible illness and pain.

Your goal is to present Wicca in the light of a dignified, serious religion. If you're doing or saying anything that doesn't support that, then *quit* it.

Taking Control of the Media

Many Wiccans have no idea how to control their media image, so they should not be talking to the media at all. They let the interviewers control the questions and manipulate the answers because they're too inexperienced and too uninformed to realize that they're being led down the primrose path. Understandable, because the interviewers are professionals. If this happens to you, remember one thing: You're talking about *your religion*. No matter what they ask you, keep it in your own mind that the subject you'll discuss is religion: not folklore, not magic, not your wardrobe, not ghosts and haunted houses.

If you can help it, do not agree to doing the interview in spooky circumstances or against an "atmospheric" background of candles in the darkness or spooky props. If the interviewers insist on compliance, refuse to grant the interview. Don't kid yourself that you're doing the religion any good by "getting the word out" no matter what compromises you have to make: All you'll be doing is sending those mixed messages. Many Wiccans agree to do these things because they figure that if *they* don't, the producers will find some witch who will—and then *that* witch will be on TV instead! This is of prime importance to some Wiccans.

Ask yourself—and ask the director or interviewer: Would this interview be different if I were a Baptist minister or a Catholic priest? Would the questions be different? Would they interview a rabbi against a black backdrop decorated with skulls? Would they ask a Methodist minister to shoot some footage in a graveyard? Are they asking about serious issues or are they asking you to be there just to provide a chill thrill?

Don't just jump in and agree to be interviewed. To some extent, you can set your own rules. Tell them up front that there are certain things you won't do, certain questions you don't want to get into. For instance, for the past couple of years I've done featured guest chats for Lycos. Lycos, especially, is great: I tell them what issues I want to avoid. I love the Lycos chats because the people who screen the questions are sensitive about issues, and they get intelligent questions. I also do radio talk shows and some call-in shows. Radio interviewers usually screen their callers, so tell the people doing the screening that there are some questions that you just won't take.

Some issues and questions to avoid are:

Nazis and the occult. You wouldn't believe how often this comes up. But you aren't there to discuss "the occult," you're there to discuss religion.

Don't get into discussions of any religion other than your own. You're not there to knock anyone else's religion, or to promote anyone else's. Fundamentalist Christians love to call in to radio shows in an attempt to turn the conversation toward their own agenda, and the call screeners usually let them through because the host wants controversy. Make it very clear that you won't talk to those people. Let them get their own show. Then *we'll* call *them!* Do you love it? "Hi! I'd just like to ask if you've considered taking Athena as your personal Goddess?"

Some Wiccans study the Bible endlessly (a waste of time if ever I saw one—most Wiccans could use the time brushing up on anthropology or history) in order to quote scripture back at fundamentalists, hoping to lure them into contradictions. What this is supposed to prove is beyond me. Forget this approach. You're not going to convince anybody of anything, and you're going to look like a couple of five-year-olds in the sandbox. What you *will* do is waste interview time that would be better used in answering real questions and talking about real issues.

Back off the entire so-called Burning Times issue, unless you know your facts, because quite a lot of what Wiccans know about it is bullshit. If you mention the "nine million dead" figure or the theory that it was a holocaust against women, you're on shaky factual ground right off the bat. The Inquisition was about heresy and the European witch hysteria dealt with diabolism. The Salem trials were about property, political control, and social disputes; none of the accused was an actual Witch, and they sure weren't Wiccans. If you're going to discuss any of this, make sure you've read quite a bit of the excellent and very available literature. (More on the Burning Times in chapter 2.)

But keep in mind that none of this has anything to do with the practice of Wicca.

Magic. I treat the discussion of magic exactly as I treat the discussion of prayer. If you know the difference between prayer as supplication to a god and spells as partnership between gods and Witches, then by all means talk about it. Limit yourself to discussing magic in a religious context, such as the relationship between magic and miracles, or the role of magic in ancient religious practices. Interviewers want to hear all about spells and hexes and curses, and if you fall into this subject, you'll find it very hard to work your way back out.

Jesus. Jesus is not part of the Wiccan religion, so why bring him into it?

Satan. Same deal. Just say we don't believe in the Devil or sin or hell.

Jehovah. Just one of the gods. And since he doesn't like to share the stage with any other gods, you might as well leave the discussion of him to those who follow him.

Demons, demon possession, and exorcism. We don't believe in this, either. Not part of Wicca.

Nature worship. Wiccans do not worship nature. We *worship* gods and work with powerful earth spirits. We *revere* nature and the earth, but certainly don't worship them.

Skyclad. If you regularly hold rituals while skyclad, then you can talk about it. If you don't, you're not qualified to bring it up. Just say you don't worship while naked. Or nekkid, either.

Harry Potter. Oh yeah. With three more books and six more movies to go, they're gonna ask you. Just tell 'em your favorite flavor of Bertie Bott's Beans and make it clear that you're not there to discuss fiction. If you like Harry, though, feel free to say so: I sure do, especially for the books' beneficial effects on children's literacy. But I strongly add that the books have nothing to do with actual Witchcraft or Wicca, something with which J. K. Rowling publicly agrees.

Frivolous Questions and Obviously Biased Interviews

Interviewers usually have a very different agenda from yours, an agenda you might not like. Probably you won't know this until the interview begins. If you find yourself being asked a lot of stupid questions in a patronizing manner, you'll just have to do the best you can or find a graceful way out. Getting mad and arguing, then storming off is strictly for Jerry Springer white-trash.

Try to find out something about the interviewer or the show or the publication before you agree to the interview. Sometimes this is difficult because you don't have time to prepare: Radio talk shows especially tend to call you to ask you to be part of the show, then tell you that they're going on the air in an hour. You usually haven't heard the show because it's on an out-of-town station. Physically being in the studio is a rarity these days. You're most likely to be on a phone hookup. In this situation, ask some questions about the show's format. What city is it being broadcast in? Is it a call-in show? Are there other guests, and who are they?

Does the producer or call screener know that there are some questions or issues that you won't talk about? Is this a church-sponsored station (yep, they call Witches all the time, and you can imagine how the interviews are going to turn out)?

Use your own judgment here. Many Wiccans won't do a show unless they know the format, and for very good reason: Lots of call-in shows are run by shock jocks, and you're the freak of the day. Remember that the show's producers have a five-second delay to bleep out anything you may say that doesn't fit the format, and that they can cut you off and back on and you'll never be aware of it. The jock is in complete control here, and after all—it's *his* show. These guys are much better at manipulating the interview than you are: They're professionals and they're paid well for it. If the interview is going badly and you're being treated with disre-spect, your only out is to make a *polite* statement that you were invited to talk about your religion, but because that doesn't seem to be the subject or the interviewer just doesn't seem to be getting the message, you're hanging up. *And hang up.* You're in a no-win situation. Don't even worry about what the jock's going to say afterward—you can't control that. Just cut your losses in the most graceful way possible and remember the experience.

Magazines and newspapers are different. You have a chance to look at the publications and decide if you'll be getting a fair inter-view. But looks are deceiving. One of the most informative stories on Wicca ran in the *Christian Science Monitor*. And one of the worst ran in that bastion of liberal thought: *Atlantic Monthly*. The *Wall Street Journal* has done articles on Wicca, and considering the crappy economy, a little magic sure couldn't hurt down on Wall Street.

Don't be afraid to ask the interviewer what the focus of the article will be. Ask who else the interviewer will be talking to, or has talked to, and what issues were raised. If he or she can't or won't answer that, there's a problem. I was once interviewed by a newspaper reporter who seemed to be overly concerned with ghosts, hauntings, and the afterlife. Since this isn't exactly the point of Wicca, I was wondering what she had in mind. It turned out that she had come straight from interviewing a pair of sensationalistic "ghostbusters" who had filled her with all kinds of horror-movie stuff about demons and exorcism. We managed to get all that out of the way very quickly, once she understood that Wicca isn't about ghosts.

A Witch experienced with interviews can usually tell which way the journalistic wind is blowing, and tailor answers accordingly. But this isn't something that first-timers can do, especially with a pro interviewer. Again, your best bet is to stick to religion and answer in that context: If it doesn't have to do with your religion, you don't have to answer it.

Remember: You're not getting paid for any of this, you're not a performer, and you're not required to answer anything. If you decide to end the interview, you can't be sued. But the wisest thing is doing what you can to minimize the chances of getting into a difficult situation. Honestly, problems don't come up all that often, but often enough so it's best to be prepared.

Usually getting interviewed is fun, provided that you stay relaxed, that you go into it with the idea that you're giving information (not delivering a long-winded lecture), that you don't lose your sense of humor, and that you remember why you're there.

You can have a good time, do the religion some good . . . and sometimes you'll get free doughnuts. It doesn't get any better than that.

8

Dealing With Discrimination

In America, a country that idealizes religious freedom, it's ridiculous that some of us constantly have to explain our religion to other people in an attempt to stave off religious discrimination. Sometimes the people you're explaining it to know zip about their own religion—they just know that yours isn't the One True Religion, like theirs is.

As I write this, a little over a month after the bombing of the World Trade Center and the Pentagon, American Muslims are desperately trying to explain that the fundamentalist Islamic terrorists do not represent the real beliefs of Islam. In this case, with hysteria running rampant, some Muslims justifiably fear for their lives. In just this short a time, there have been some nasty—and even fatal—incidents carried out by people who consider themselves God-fearing and patriotic. It doesn't even occur to them that the two don't necessarily go together. You can be a patriot without God even entering into the equation. If that weren't true, there wouldn't be so many Wiccans (not to mention atheists) in the armed forces.

Religious discrimination stems from ignorance. To the majority of Americans, if you're not a Christian, there's something suspect about your religion. With the number of Jews in this country, it's scandalous that anti-Semitism still exists, but there are always assholes willing to scrawl on synagogue walls, and they're not always your basic drooling inbred skinheads or Kluxers, either. The numbers of Muslims have been growing for years, but as a nation we still know zip about their beliefs. We just don't bother to find out. Fer chrissakes, there's still discrimination against *Catholics*.

Americans in general are pretty apathetic about religion. The only time most of us come into personal contact with it is when somebody gets married or dies, or at Easter, Christmas, Yom Kippur, or Samhain. (Yeah, we've got 'em, too, so don't feel smug.) So asking us to learn about other religions when we don't even have time for our own is asking a lot.

Given this apathy, it's easy for the loudest mouth and the biggest bank account to be allowed to form religious opinion and policy in this country. And no one is louder, and has more money to publicize their rigid views, than the so-called religious right. I find it difficult to believe that someone like Pat Robertson doesn't know the basic beliefs of Wicca, but to listen to his past rants about us being Satan's allies, you'd think he'd never made it past fifth grade. (Although now that it's expedient for him, he's getting behind Zionism—and if the Israelis fall for *that* one, you'll see a Hasidic rabbi eat a BLT on toast with a glass of milk.)

Followers of the televangelists like Robertson and Falwell usually know only what they're told by the TV preacher of their choice, and regard other religions as sinful and invalid, their practitioners as people to be converted and therefore "saved." And what the fundamentalist televangelists have been preaching about Wicca is so biased as to be outright lies.

Some fundamentalists can justify the most evil actions by insisting that they're doing it for God, or to "save souls." These are the people who actively discriminate, who are ignorant of any religion outside their own cult (and fundamentalism is a cult, never doubt that), and who see people who practice other religions as somewhat less than human until they convert. *Hint:* Anyone who insists on calling himself "a good Christian" usually isn't. Real Christians are mortified by these nutcases. And please don't judge Christians by these fundamentalists: Some mainstream Christians and ministers have been good friends to Wiccans, as we'll see in chapter 9, on activism.

Most of these TV preachers go on and on about praying in schools and the new "faith-based initiatives" ideas. The problem with these programs is that they discriminate. For instance, "prayer in school," to the conservative Christians who are pushing it, means *Christian* prayer and no other. Don't hold your breath to see a little Voudoun kid sacrificing a chicken to the *loa* at school prayer time anytime soon, no matter how ancient and valid the religion is. The "faith-based initiative" proponents have already made it clear that some religions need not apply. Especially Wicca.

From all this, you might have guessed what I'm saying: Discrimination exists. The forms it takes range from subtle to extreme, the perpetrators run from stupid jerks to educated people who should know better.

Okay, let me give you a situation that, unfortunately, is *not* a hypothetical one.

A Pagan was asking for opinions from other Pagans on an Internet newsgroup. She said that a coworker and good friend of hers was a strict Christian who didn't know that the woman was . . . well, Pagan, and that her friend often said derogatory things about Pagans. The woman noted that the casual manner in which these things were said was what hurt the most, but she just gritted her teeth and said nothing. Finally, the Christian said something that really stung, and the Pagan was wondering how to handle it. Another thing that bothered her was that the Christian occasionally sent officewide e-mails with cheery "Jesus Loves You" messages. The Pagan wanted to mention to her that not everyone shared her religious beliefs, but finally decided that it wasn't worth making a fuss about, although it still bothered her.

You know what disturbs me the most about this?

The fact that the Christian felt perfectly at ease to express her religious views publicly, yet the Pagan felt constrained to hide her own religion while putting up with this. (Just as an aside, using company e-mail for religious or any other non-work-related purpose is something that human resource departments don't like.) And the Pagan had managed to convince herself that expressing her feelings and beliefs wasn't worthwhile.

Why? Why do so many of us feel that we just can't say anything about such subtle discrimination, even if it hurts us personally? Is it because we know that what *they* believe is accepted as a valid religion, and what *we* believe is considered flaky? Are we afraid that we'll lose friends or our jobs, or that we'll become the butt of jokes—or even objects of fear—if we speak out, even in the mildest of ways?

And the worst part of this is that the Pagan always has "rational" reasons for not objecting: It would create a fuss at work or home, it would make people uncomfortable, it would cause bad feelings. *Bad feelings?* Are you joking? It's already caused bad feelings— *yours!* Why should your feelings come second to theirs? This is not selfishness, this is the preservation of self and belief. This is your own relationship with your deity we're talking about.

Actually, I was wrong about "the worst part." The worst part is that all this Pagan's fears are justified. She just might lose her job, her friends, maybe her kids if some do-gooder decides to complain to Social Services about a "satanist" mom . . . These things have happened. At best, if it becomes known that she's Wiccan or Pagan, her coworkers will treat her differently. Mention that you're a Wiccan to the average person and you can count on the wary, stone-faced response. They even draw back a bit, as if you'll contaminate them or suddenly grow fangs and take off their face. Great for your self-esteem.

It's real easy to honor the Goddess at home and at Pagan gatherings. If you're an out-of-the-closet Wiccan, why are you letting her—and you—be tromped on anywhere else? That's part of the reason why so many Pagans attend Pagan conferences and events: We can express ourselves without fear. But you know what? We should be able to do that anywhere, at any time, just as Christians do when they call for a "word of prayer." The next time a Christian feels she has the right to open or close a nonreligious meeting with "Could we all just pause for a word of prayer?" there's no reason why you shouldn't object, or at least opt out. In the first place, if this is a workplace, it's inappropriate. If someone feels the need to pray, why should that involve everyone else? Or, if you're feeling frisky, wait until the "word of prayer" is finished and ask everyone to join you in a word of thanks to Diana. Or—my favorite—when everyone else says "amen," you say "So mote it be." Heh, heh . . .

These things aren't minor; they're the stuff we shouldn't let just pass by. Why not? Because when we do, we are reinforcing (even to ourselves) the belief that our religion is not as important as theirs. We're also letting ingrained ideas about us continue to flourish, which is bad enough, but I'm more concerned about what you're doing to your own sense of pride and self-esteem.

And I'm not telling you that it's easy to speak out. What I'm telling you is that you should conquer your fear and do it anyway, if you possibly can without jeopardizing your job and your family.

You don't need to make a big-ass statement or stage a demonstration. For instance, if I were the Pagan cited earlier, I'd just mention to my Christian friend that I was a Pagan and that these opinions of hers hurt my feelings. (Don't ever underestimate the power of guilt!) If I wanted to take it further, I'd offer to explain anything about my religion that she wanted to know—but not at work.

As for the e-mails, you could reply to the e-mailer that not everyone believes as he or she does and that the office is inappropriate for this. If that doesn't work, forward the e-mail to the HR department. That's what they're there for, and because of the Equal Opportunity Commission guidelines, almost every company has a policy against proselytizing at work. Don't assume that you're the only one who's uncomfortable with it.

By the way . . . the remark that the coworker made that was the final, ultimate last straw for the Pagan? "You know, Halloween is actually a Christian holiday that the Pagans took over."

How the Pagan kept a straight face is beyond me.

All this assumes that you are able to be open and up front about your religious preference. You may not be. You may work in a company or a position that would definitely fire you, or make you so uncomfortable that you'd have to leave. (Yes, this happens. It's illegal, but it happens all the time.) You may have to consider the feelings of children or other family members who might be harmed if it was known that you are a Witch or Wiccan. No one expects you to put yourself or your livelihood at risk, nor should they. What I'm saying is that if you *can* speak out, exercise your freedom and *do* speak out. You should not have to take religious abuse.

Another reason that people are reluctant to speak out is that they just don't feel like getting involved in a long, draining discussion. For some of us, it seems like we're continually saying the same things over and over: No, we don't believe in Satan; no, we don't believe in animal or human sacrifice; no, we don't run around in the woods naked; yes, we're an earth-centered religion; no, we're not interested in hearing about Jesus.

It's especially frustrating when you have the feeling (and you can trust your intuition on this) that the people you're taking valuable time to educate only want some amusing anecdote to tell their friends later.

Part-Time Pagans

Some Pagans have a saying that we paraphrased from gays: "Coming out of the broom closet." We're constantly asking if someone's out of the broom closet, or referring to ourselves as out of the broom closet or out only to certain people or out, but not out at work. Depends on the circumstances. Some of us are in and out of the closet so often that we should install a revolving door.

Take this simple test. Ask yourself:

1. If I was getting married to another Pagan, would we have a Pagan ceremony and *only* a Pagan ceremony, or would we agree to a second one in our parents' religion, and not just for the possibility of extra presents? (Not that I am for a second discounting the "extra presents" benefit.)
2. If we had children, would we have them baptized or christened just to placate our families? Would we take them to Sunday school or church because we "don't have the right to decide their religion for them"? (If you, as a parent, don't have the right to give your kids religious training, then who does?)
3. What kind of religious ceremony am I going to have when I die, seeing as I'm not going to be around to make the arrangements and may have to just take what my family wants, and besides I'm dead, what do I care by then?

I know that these are hard questions. They deal with everyday life issues, not with high-minded theoretical debates about the nature of religious belief. How we handle these passages in our lives means something about what we believe and how strongly we believe it. Our aim in these ceremonies is to become closer with our gods, making the statement publicly and privately that we want to share these events with our deities and ask for their blessings and protection in our lives. We're also making a statement of love and honor to them. If you're going to leave out the gods, you might as well get married down at the local courthouse.

For instance, if you're being married in the Episcopal Church, or getting your kid baptized, you're going to have to recite the creed, which begins: "I believe in one God, the Father Almighty, maker of heaven and earth, and in Jesus Christ . . ."

Do you really? Then why are you saying so? At one stroke, you've lied to one god and denied the others. And you're actually going to go do your next full moon ritual and ask for protection and help from a goddess or god you've just said doesn't exist? You'd better hope that you're not working with goddesses like Kali, the Morrigan, or Hecate. Those girls aren't likely to take it lightly.

This is also highly disrespectful of the church you're doing it in. If your family members try to force you or guilt you into having these ceremonies in church, ask them if they think so little of their religion that they don't mind your lying to the priest or preacher about your belief—or the lack of it. (They might not care. They may think it's worse if the neighbors talk about your not having your ceremony in church.)

This will probably come as a shock to them because, generally, most Christians don't even think about what they're saying during religious rituals. They just say it because they've always said it: It's long ago ceased to have any meaning. Still, even if they don't mind you lying to the priest, rabbi, or preacher, I can almost guarantee you that the cleric will mind. Be honest with him (or her, as may be the case with Protestants and Jews) and tell him that you don't believe in the religion or that Jehovah is the only God around, that you don't believe that Jesus was the Messiah or the son of God, *and you're not going to say that you do*. If you can work something out, fine. If not, tell your family that the priest refuses to perform the ceremony.

Bear in mind that most priests or ministers will either give you up as a lost cause and feel that at least they can "save" the child (if you're having a baptism or christening), or they'll view the ceremony as an occasion to "save" you and/or make an example of you to the congregation. Some of these guys don't take rejection of their beliefs very well. And to be fair, if you're consenting to a Christian wedding ceremony just so you can have a nice room to do your wedding in, you deserve any disapproval you get. That's why there are hotel function rooms, nondenominational chapels, and catering halls that don't require religious ceremonies. You can have a big wedding or a small one and don't have to abide by the church's rules or the whims of some priest.

You may be unaware of this, but in many states getting married does *not* require a preacher or priest. Not even a ceremony. All that is required is that the two of you declare your intention to be married, and that you do it in front of witnesses and someone authorized to record the marriage for the state—like a justice of the peace. Or a Wiccan priestess or priest who has been ordained by a legally recognized religious organization. The Universal Life Church has long been a traditional avenue for Wiccans: Their ordination is accepted as legal in all fifty states. The Covenant of the Goddess, the Church of All Worlds, and the Aquarian Tabernacle Church also ordain legal Wiccan clergy, although they have some stricter requirements than the ULC, which has none. Be wary of small, local Wiccan organizations that claim to have registered with the state as a legal religion: Many of them have actually not met the requirements. Or they get involved in some Witch War and disband, or banish half the coven. You don't want your ministerial credentials subject to whim.

Frankly, if you're old enough to get married or have a child, you should be of an age where you make your own decisions rather than letting your parents or family decide for you.

Most Wiccans who agree to these ceremonies excuse it by saying that not getting married in church or not having their child baptized will create a rift in the family, or will cause a row. Once again, it's the Wiccan who is expected to give in and show "reason" about what is actually an unreasonable request: that you abandon your own religious beliefs to abide by someone else's. The assumption is that your religion is flaky while theirs is real. Yours is a fad you'll grow out of while theirs is enduring.

We've turned weddings and christenings into social occasions, completely glossing over the religious implications. When the families insist on baptisms, christenings, and big weddings, they're not thinking of the religious meaning: They're thinking of the photo ops and the party afterward. They're thinking of all the people they'll invite and what they'll all wear, and how impressed the guests will be. If you've ever been involved in a big wedding, you know that more anguish is involved with the color of the bridesmaids' gowns than with the religious ritual.

If you're a Wiccan and you want a handfasting, but your parents want a church wedding, maybe instead of a wedding you should have your handfasting by invitation only, attended only by those who share your faith or at least respect it; then have a big reception afterward for everybody. Nobody says you have to have the reception on the same day as the handfasting, either.

But What About the Kids?

Again, ask yourself a basic question: *Would I want my child to be a Wiccan?* If the answer is no, then you shouldn't be one either. Why are you practicing a religion that you don't respect? If you think so little of Wicca that you don't want to raise your kids according to its principles, then maybe you should think about finding a religion that suits you better, and that you can respect.

Kids are raised as Catholics and Jews and Muslims and Protestants every day. I daresay you were probably raised as one or the other, or at least you and your parents considered yourselves to belong to a particular religion, even if you never went to church or synagogue or mosque.

If you believe in the principles of Wicca, then by all means teach it to your kids. Kids need a belief system, especially when they're preteens. It gives them an anchor, a set of guidelines for behavior; this kind of thing is comforting to kids, who haven't yet had enough life experience to form their own guidelines.

Have your child Wiccaned. It's a lovely ceremony, and will give your child a good start, with the protection of the gods and spirits, and the good wishes of the people who love the child.

Teach the kid the basic principles of Wicca, especially the Rede and the Threefold Law. I can't think of a better guide for behavior than "harm none" and "what goes around, comes around." Karma and reincarnation are more comforting to kids than that "heaven and hell" and "sin and guilt" crapola they're going to hear everywhere else. And trust me, your kid's not going to be ignorant of other religions, especially Christianity: It's part of the culture. But where else is your child going to learn *your* religion if not from you?

Take your child to the major rituals for the Sabbats. If you're in a coven, devise some rituals just for children, or help the kids devise their own rituals. Wiccans, for all our lip service to children, are very lax in including them in a meaningful way in the ceremonies of our religion. Okay, yeah, Beltane is a fertility festival and some covens have some fairly explicit rituals for the Sabbat. Big Effin' Deal: Have a pre-Beltane Maypole for the kids, let them learn about fertility by planting trees or flowers and potted plants. Heck, May is the prime season for planting pumpkin seeds for Samhain: You can make a nice family tradition out of saving the Halloween jack o' lantern seeds to plant in the spring. All the Sabbats were based in agriculture anyway; that's what they were for. And make sure your kids know the difference between Samhain (religious) and Halloween (fun!). You have at least eight chances a year to teach your child all about the religion and why we do the things we do. Why pass up the opportunity to do something so meaningful together?

If the relatives bitch about this, they're going to have to suck it up and get over it. They're *your* kids. If the grandparents insist on taking your children to church, they really have no right to do it: They had their chance with you, you were *their* responsibility, and your kids are *your* responsibility. I think you can work out for yourself the kind of comments that little Wiccan-raised kids are likely to hear from some good Christians and their "pastors," and they aren't going to be complimentary to your religion. Many Christians are fairly tactless when it comes to hurting the feelings of little Wiccan kids. At the very least, they'll feel sorry for the godless little heathens, being brought up with what they consider no religion at all. This is where you're going to have to put your foot down and tell your relatives that you're raising your child in the religion that you yourself practice, and that you're happy with it.

If your child *asks* to go, that's a different story. And don't think it isn't going to come up. Their school friends are likely to invite them to some church function sooner or later. Don't be surprised if your child decides to be a Baptist or Catholic or something for a while: Kids try on religions like they try on new sneakers. Either it will pass or it won't. If it doesn't, and the kid really likes being a Methodist (probably to get in on all those Bean Suppers), then your child has made an informed religious decision. Informed, because he knows the religion of Wicca and decided it isn't for him. We have religious freedom in this country, and it applies to kids, too. As long as your child isn't joining a dangerous religious cult that requires her to shave her head and annoy people at the airport and the mall, she'll probably be fine.

Of course, if you want to *ensure* that your kids become Witches, raise them Catholic. For some reason, an inordinate number of Catholics head straight to Wicca as soon as they get away from home. And if they went to Catholic school, the chances of their becoming Wiccan are even higher. Our high number of Catholic converts is always a source of amusement to Wiccans. Probably it's because the snacks are better: We usually have big feasts, and they only get those little crackers. The Catholic Church is having real problems these days finding priests, but we have no problem getting Wiccans from the Roman rank and file. Maybe the Vatican should start recruiting from the Covenant of the Goddess: Who knows?

Kids and Magic

When Silver RavenWolf came out with her "Teen Witch Kit," there were Wiccans all up in arms, saying that their concern was that kids just weren't prepared to do magic, that they didn't know what they were fooling around with, that they could be harmed.

Oh, please. I don't know what was in Silver's kit, but as far as kids doing magic, we're talking beginner's folk magic here, not invoking powerful deities or performing ceremonial magic workings. And if you're a Wiccan parent, you'd be supervising your child's spells anyway.

Exactly what is it that Wiccans do that could cause harm to children? Maybe the problem is that if any child can do magic, that sure puts a puncture in the egotistical High Priestess Lady PowerWitch, who uses her so-called occult knowledge and dangerous powers to impress people with how "advanced in the Craft" she is.

Let me tell you: Kids *love* doing magic! I know this for sure because I wrote a whole book of beginning magic just for kids, complete with a discussion of magical ethics, and kids wrote to me telling me how much they enjoyed it. And I mean young kids like eight and ten, even though the book was meant for young teens. (I got letters from adults who liked it, too.) The children had no problem understanding the Threefold Law and the "harm none" rules and the broader implications of both. They also caught right on to the definition of manipulative magic and free will—something that many adult Wiccans seem to find difficult, mainly because they're always looking for a way around it.

Kids are really good at magic. And it's good for them. For one thing, it empowers kids to know that they have the powers of gods on their side, and that the gods will help them better understand themselves. They're great at inventing spells and rituals, learning about the various magical colors and stones and herbs, keeping magical journals, making amulets and protective charms. It gives them a sense of control over their lives, an important thing in times when kids can feel so powerless. Understanding what spirits are and how they work also helps kids get over the fear of "ghosts and demons" that a predominantly Christian superstitious culture ingrains in children. Personally, I'd rather have my kid hanging a protective charm on the bedpost than saying that "if I should die before I wake" stuff at night. And some people wonder why their kids have sleep disorders.

If magic and spells are, as Wiccans like to say, forms of prayer, then why are some Wiccans so against kids learning magic? Magic and ritual allow children to honor the gods and come to know the powers in themselves.

Coming Out at Work

If you don't feel comfortable coming out at work, then there is no earthly reason why people you work with should know you're a Wiccan, any more than they should know that you're a Catholic or a Jew. Religion of any sort has no part in the workplace; in fact, it's illegal for your employers to even ask you about it. Want proof? Read the Civil Rights Act of 1964, which prohibits discrimination according to, among other things, religion. However, as of this writing, the "faith-based initiative" political program would exempt religious organizations from the Civil Rights Act. In other words, if you work for, say, Methodist Hospital, they could require that you be a Methodist. Or that you become one. Conversion or unemployment! No wonder the religious right loves the idea.

What if someone at work *does* ask you about your religious affiliation? Just say that your religion is something you keep private. They may suspect you're a Godless Atheist, but there's no law against that, either.

9

Wiccan Activism, Protecting Your Rights, and the IRS

To be a bona fide religious belief entitled to protection under either the First Amendment or Title VII, a belief must be sincerely held, and within the believer's own scheme of things religious.
Civil Rights Act of 1964, USCA Const. Amend 1: Civil Rights Act 1964 701 et seq., 717 as amended 42 USCA 2000–16

Wiccans like to characterize our struggle as one for religious freedom. This is nonsense. Last time I checked, every U.S. citizen already has religious freedom: says so right there in the Constitution. If we're denied our basic rights under the Constitution on the grounds of religion, we have the law on our side.

What we *don't* have is an across-the-board recognition of our religion as a valid one. We're constantly having to go to court on a case-by-case basis, mainly because many lawmakers and law enforcement officials don't know the law. Even judges and elected officials have no idea that Wicca is a religion, although it has been such for almost twenty years. When the president of the United States says publicly that he doesn't believe that Witchcraft is a religion, we're in trouble. Or he is. You'd think this guy would know the law, or at least have advisers who can keep him from speaking out on issues of which he is ignorant

Before you engage in any kind of activism, or go off on the fact that your religious rights have been violated, you might want to know what some of those rights are. So for those of you who haven't paid attention in civics class, which includes most of us, let's start off with the biggie, the First Amendment:

> Congress shall make no law respecting an establishment of religion, or prohibiting the free exercise thereof; or abridging the freedom of speech, or of the press; or the right of the people peaceably to assemble, and to petition the Government for a redress of grievances.

That's it, short, sweet, and guaranteeing your religious freedom. But there are a couple of important points that need a little expanding.

The Free Exercise Clause of the First Amendment

The First Amendment specifically guarantees that "Congress shall make no law . . . prohibiting the free exercise" of religion. According to the Supreme Court, this means that the government can't interfere with or attempt to regulate your religious beliefs, including forcing you to affirm ideas or beliefs offensive to your own religious beliefs. It also prohibits discrimination against a person whose beliefs are contrary to those held by anyone else. Most important for Wiccans, religious beliefs need not be acceptable, logical, or comprehensible to others in order to merit First Amendment protection. This last bit was a big help in *Dettmer v. Landon,* which we'll look at a little more closely later.

Freedom of Association

Freedom of association is implicitly guaranteed by the First Amendment and has the same protection as other First Amendment freedoms. Freedom of association protects the right of individuals to gather without hindrance for purposes of practicing religion. This freedom is extended to all religious groups, including those that hold unpopular, controversial, and unorthodox beliefs. Does this describe us or *what?*

This being America and Americans being the literal and contrary folk that we are, the First Amendment has been subjected to various federal court interpretations throughout the years. For a really complete discussion of the implications and baroque interpretations of the First Amendment, you can go to www.findlaw.com. This is a great beginning resource when you're interested in finding out more about your rights and the laws pertaining to them. But remember: When you've got a serious constitutional problem, nothing is a substitute for a really sharp constitutional lawyer. And when one saves your ass, you'll think twice about lawyer jokes.

The Fourteenth Amendment

Section 1. All persons born or naturalized in the United States and subject to the jurisdiction thereof, are citizens of the United States and of the State wherein they reside. No State shall make or enforce any law which shall abridge the privileges or immunities of citizens of the United States; nor shall any State deprive any person of life, liberty, or property, without due process of law; nor deny to any person within its jurisdiction the equal protection of the laws.

This amendment guarantees that you have the same rights as everyone else: We all get equal protection under the law. And if your state has laws that conflict with your freedoms under the First Amendment—not just your religious freedom, but it includes that, too—then your state is in violation of the Fourteenth Amendment. Your state can't make or enforce any state or local laws that restrict your First Amendment rights.

Dettmer v. Landon *and Its Importance to Wiccans*

Since 1986, Wiccans have relied on the appellate decision in *Dettmer v. Landon* to secure their religious rights. This case was decided in the U.S. District Court for the Eastern District of Virginia on September 4, 1986.

Briefly, Herbert Dettmer was doing time at Powhatan Correctional Center in Virginia and studying Wicca through the Church of Wicca's correspondence courses. He asked for some basic tools: candles, incense, a white hooded robe, a hollow statue of a goddess or god, an egg timer to time his meditations, and sea salt or sulfur to inscribe a protective Circle. The prison refused, so Dettmer sued. The prison had some logical reasons for refusing: The egg timer could be used as a detonator or the hollow statue to hide contraband, for instance. Dettmer said he could compromise with a digital alarm clock, and offered to make similar concessions on the other items, so that prison security would be satisfied. The prison still refused, but this time they said that if Dettmer could provide them with written proof, through doctrine, that the full practice of the rite, plus the items, was a required tenet of his faith, then the prison would reconsider.

Dettmer went all the way through all four levels of the required grievance procedures, and he still didn't get his stuff. So on October 29, 1984 (good magical choice, Herb!), he filed a suit alleging that the Virginia Department of Corrections had deprived him of his freedom of religion.

He won. The court held that the Church of Wicca was a religion, and it ordered the correctional center to give Dettmer his things.

And here it gets really hairy. *The government appealed,* saying that the Church of Wicca was *not* a religion, and was therefore *not* entitled to First Amendment protection. *And even if it was a religion,* it still didn't require that he needed all those things to practice it. *And even if it did,* he wasn't gonna get them because (surprise!) they endangered prison security. Which was the whole argument in the first place.

The government still didn't believe the Church of Wicca was a real religion. Instead, they said, it's a conglomeration of occultism, including faith healing, self-hypnosis, tarot card reading, and spell casting. It's illogical and internally inconsistent.*

That argument didn't work, since the Supreme Court had held in a previous case that religious beliefs need not be acceptable, logical, consistent, or comprehensible to others to merit First Amendment protection.† This is very important for Wicca: Just because someone doesn't understand our religion, that doesn't mean it isn't one. I don't understand transubstantiation in Catholicism, but I'm not saying Catholicism isn't a real religion.

Actually, the government did us all a favor by these assertions, because it allowed a federal court to determine whether the Church of Wicca was a valid religion, protected by the free exercise clause. What had to be determined here was whether or not the Church of Wicca's members took the same comfort in their religion as Catholics, Jews, or Protestants took in theirs. For that, the court went to a previous case, *United States v. Seeger,* and sure enough, according to that decision, we're the same as anyone else, religiously speaking. (A note here, if you're ever in trouble on religious grounds: Make sure that your lawyer is familiar with the *Seeger* decision.‡)

The government also raised an objection to meditation as part of the Wiccan religious experience. They said it was simply a way to master positive thinking and produce contentment. Dettmer testified that he meditated in order to call down power from the supreme being and other deities. The court upheld that meditation is indeed religious, again according to a previous case.§

So here are the questions: *Are we a religion?* Yes. The district court found that members of the Church of Wicca adhere to a

---

*Well, damn . . . we all knew *that.*

†*Thomas v. Review Board,* 450 U.S. 707, 714, 67 L. Ed. 2d 624, 101 S. Ct. 1425 (1981). Don't even bother to make sense of these citations, but if you ever get in a tight spot, mention them to your lawyer.

‡*United States v. Seeger,* 380 U.S. 163, 1666, 13 L. Ed. 2d 733, 85 S. Ct. 850 (1964).

§Malnak, 592 F. 2d at 198 n.2 and 199.

fairly complex set of doctrines relating to the spiritual aspect of their lives, the same as members of other religions. The Church of Wicca believes in another world and has a broad concern for improving the quality of life for others. *Are we entitled to the same protection as other religions, under the First and Fourteenth Amendments?* You bet your ass. *Did Dettmer get his stuff?* Yes and no. He didn't get the candles, incense, or salt, but he could have an unhooded robe, a quartz clock, and a solid, lightweight statue.

The Drawbacks of *Dettmer v. Landon*

Personally, if I was in court and had to rely solely on *Dettmer v. Landon,* I'd hate to bet the ranch on the outcome, simply because of the language of the decision.

If you're a member of the Church of Wicca, you can breathe a sigh of relief. If you're not, *Dettmer* alone might not get you a satisfactory verdict. Still, this case was a federal decision and set a precedent, so if you've got a decent lawyer, it will definitely help you, especially since it involves other previous court decisions.

But there's no denying that *Dettmer* refers specifically to the Church of Wicca, not "Witchcraft" or "Wicca." It always worries me when Wiccans and Wiccan organizations confidently acclaim that "Witchcraft is a legal religion," because if they're assuming that *Dettmer* specifically says that, they're wrong. I believed that too, for years, until I started digging into the language of the decision. The only previous exposure I'd had to *Dettmer* was through a booklet issued by the Witches' League for Public Awareness in 1989. The booklet had good intentions, but made way too many assumptions, the worst in making a specific statement that the district court "ruled that Witchcraft is a legitimate religion . . ." It did no such thing: There is no mention of "Witchcraft" in the *Dettmer* ruling. Just because the WLPA and other organizations may say that "Wicca" and "Witchcraft" are the same thing doesn't guarantee that the law does. In fact, many Witches (not Wiccans) are very vocal in insisting that they are *not* the same thing, which may be shooting themselves in the feet if they ever land in court.

This is one more reason to consult a lawyer if you have a legal problem with the practice of your faith. Do not get your advice strictly from Wiccan books, Wiccan Web sites, or your coven. Any of these may be a great help and comfort, but they're not lawyers. And if someone in your coven *is* a lawyer and is taking your case to trial, it's best if he or she specializes in constitutional law.

One more advantage that we have is that *Dettmer* has already raised and answered the issue of inconsistency in the religion: For instance, no two covens are exactly the same, although they're both Wiccan. The Supreme Court ruled that these differences don't mean that a religion is invalid, saying, "It is not within the judicial function and judicial competence to inquire whether the petitioner or [another practitioner] more correctly perceived the commands of their common faith. Courts are not arbiters of scriptural interpretation."* For which we can all thank the Goddess, because the last thing we need is an eighty-nine-year-old conservative Baptist judge in someplace like Tennessee or Arkansas interpreting the meaning of the Great Rite.

Remember: If you're having legal troubles because of your religion, or you've been discriminated against because of it, your best organizational ally in almost all cases is the American Civil Liberties Union. Despite what some politicians and conservative radio shock jocks want you to believe, the ACLU has no political agenda other than upholding the Constitution and the civil rights of citizens. They'll defend anybody whose rights have been threatened, no matter what side of the political fence they're on: They've defended "freedom riders" and other workers for racial equality during the 1960s, and they've defended the Klan's right to free assembly—just because practically everybody hates the Klan doesn't mean they don't get the same protection as every other citizen. Plenty of people don't like Wiccans either, and think that we shouldn't be allowed to gather for our Sabbats. At one point,

*Also from *Thomas v. Review Board,* and *Barrett v. Virginia,* 689 F.2d 1345 (4th Cir. 1982).

the ACLU almost defended me: I was intending to sue the state of Connecticut over an old law that prohibited things like tarot reading and divination, on the grounds that divination is part of my religion. Thus, the law could be used to abridge the rights of Wiccans. The Connecticut ACLU offered to help. Fortunately, the state repealed the law, so an ACLU defense—or any other—was no longer necessary. (A big gasp of relief from me, you betcha!) The ACLU has a very informative Web site at http://www.aclu.org.

Another friend you might not know you have is People for the American Way, a watchdog group in Washington, D.C. What do they watch? The religious right and their political allies, for one thing. You might recall that in the aftermath of the September 11 tragedy, Jerry Falwell asserted that the terrorist attack was caused by gays, Pagans, the ACLU, and People for the American Way, among others. (His sidekick, Pat Robertson, nodded enthusiastically and said, "I concur.") Frankly, any group that Jerry Falwell hates is probably doing a good job of keeping his political influence-mongering in check, so we might want to support that group. The People for the American Way Foundation conducts research, legal, and educational work. If you're involved in activism, you need to know about this group, because the research information they can provide is priceless. Their Web site is http://www.pfaw.org.

Activism: Effectively Working for Change

The whole object of activism is not simply to get publicity for your cause, it's to get public *support* for your cause, so that you can effect change. You also need the support of lawmakers and those who influence public policy. Publicity alone won't cut it, especially publicity that makes Witches look silly. You don't want to be known as "those clowns protesting so-and-such"; you want to make people think, *Those Wiccans may have a point.*

The most effective Wiccan activists know how to work the system. They don't confront officials while wearing the robes and jewelry as if it were battle armor. When you walk into a roomful of suits and you're wearing the Semi-Official Black Getup, they're so busy dealing with how you look that they don't even hear half of what you're saying. You might as well be reciting the alphabet in Greek for the first half hour. And forget about being taken seriously: Who takes a walking fairy tale character seriously? The entire outfit is usually worn to be confrontational anyway: Most Wiccans walk into meetings with non-Wiccans with a built-in chip on the shoulder, all ready to take offense. And jeeze laweeze, when you're talking to the press, *quit the whining.*

Much Wiccan activism has been purely reactive. This is understandable: We've had to defend the religion, and this probably isn't going to stop anytime soon. But we need to start expanding our influence, taking a good hard look at the community and asking, *Okay, what's missing? How can I contribute? What would be good for Wiccans and also benefit the community, and what can I do about it? Would other Wiccans, and maybe other groups, join in the effort?*

Much Wiccan "activism" involves protecting the financial investment of individuals, such as the right of a store to open or stay open. And while this is an important issue, it doesn't affect the community as a whole, but only a select part of it. Many of these cases have more to do with property values and rising rents than with discrimination, although one outrageous case comes to mind wherein the occult store's landlord got jittery because the local fundamentalists started picketing and criticizing him for renting space to those ungodly folks. He showed up at the store with a couple of preachers and evicted the Witches.

Yes, these particular battles have to be fought, but we also need to start painting on a wider canvas. The legal issues of Wiccan groups that are being denied the use of public facilities (such as public parks) for ritual are also important: If the Witches can't use it for religious purposes, then neither can the Lutherans or the Buddhists or the local Baptist church picnickers and prayer-meeters. You'd be surprised to find out that many mainstream churches are on our side in issues like this, for just this reason.

Even old Pat Robertson has been known to defend certain of our rights, because he knows that his own are inseparable from ours.

Wiccan organizations are hampered by a lack of money: There aren't a lot of rich contributors standing in line for Wiccan causes, especially if they can't see a solid plan as to how the money is going to be used to the greatest effect. Nobody's going to give you a grant to protest some stupid movie that's going to be forgotten in six months, especially if that's all your organization seems to do. The Wiccan world is full of impressively named groups that pop up every once in a while to hold a press conference, then pop back into obscurity or inactivity.

If you're thinking of joining an activist group, first find out what it has done, and what its track record is. And that track record should not consist of merely urging people to write letters or circulating Internet petitions or putting up a Web site saying, "We support so-and-so in his legal battle." That's not activism, that's reporting. (Not that reporting the news and keeping people informed isn't important, but it does not constitute taking action for religious rights.) Find out exactly what they mean by "support" and if that support was wanted or needed. Sometimes the last thing an embattled Wiccan embroiled in a legal nightmare wants is publicity. And sadly, some of these Web sites and organizations simply use the case to bolster their own reputations as activists.

Two Success Stories From the Front Lines

There are lots of courageous Wiccans out there, fighting court battles and local ordinances and all forms of discrimination, but I'm limiting this discussion to just two cases. Frankly, I could go on for hundreds of pages about the court cases won by Wiccans, and if you want more, there are great Web sites that detail the cases.

These cases are very good examples of how to get things done while bolstering the impression of the religion. The Wiccans involved did everything right, and while the victories are important, so is the method by which they were achieved.

Dallas, Texas, is a bastion of hard-core religious conservatism. It's been all but controlled by the Southern Baptist Convention for decades. So you can imagine how difficult it would be for Wicca to be recognized there as a valid religion.

But it's in Dallas that Wicca has made some significant advances.

Two Wiccan activists, Bryan Lankford, high priest of the Order of the Inner Circle and a national officer of Covenant of the Goddess, and Maeven Eller, who runs Betwixt and Between, an interfaith community center whose membership is about 80 to 90 percent Pagans, decided that Wiccan children should have equal rights when it came to school holidays. Bryan has a particular interest in this because he and his wife, Anastasia, have two daughters and they're a Wiccan family.

Bryan and Maeven worked with the Religious Task Force of the Dallas Independent School District to have the Wiccan Sabbats added to the school calendar of religious holidays. Four holidays are on the calendar now; all eight should be added in the next revision.

What's important about this is that it has implications that will reach farther than just Dallas. The First Amendment Center looks to the Dallas school district for setting precedents in religious rights for schoolchildren, so the Dallas schools may set a model for the rest of the country.

What this means for Wiccan children is not so much that they automatically get Samhain off, but that holidays like Samhain are officially recognized, and a child *can* take that day off with a note from his or her parents.

The validation for Wiccan children—and for Wiccans in general—is enormous, both for Wicca as a religion and for the psychological and emotional reinforcement it provides our kids.

Maeven's next project is to assure the children's right to wear pentacles and other religious symbols to school. In some places,

Jewish children aren't allowed to wear the Star of David, either. "We want to set precedents that will stick," she said.

The most high-profile victory in Dallas, though, involved Bryan's giving the invocation to open a session of the Dallas City Council. Usually this is a regular duty shared by the ministers of Dallas's interfaith council, Thanks-Giving Square.

As Betwixt and Between's interfaith minister, Bryan was extended an invitation to join Thanks-Giving Square by a local Baptist minister, the Reverend Roy Harrell, vice president and chaplain of the group. The Reverend Harrell had given the city a list of ministers from several other faiths, hoping to emphasize the religious diversity in Dallas. Thanks-Giving Square ministers share the duty of opening the city council meetings, on a rotating schedule. When Bryan joined, he was automatically added to the schedule.

When Bryan's turn came around and he was due to deliver the invocation, things got suspicious. City Secretary Shirley Acy said she was told by the mayor's office to cancel the invitation, saying she was told that a council member's pastor would give Wednesday's invocation instead. She also said that she didn't know who would lead the prayer.

However, Bryan's replacement, the Reverend Gerald Britt Jr. of Dallas, said that Acy called "a few days ago" and asked him to give the invocation. No council member belongs to his church, he said. "I'd been invited several times and had to cancel," said the Reverend Britt. "I figured they were giving me another chance."

Actually, what had happened was that some local fundamentalists and a radio call-in show had gotten wind of the situation and urged people to call city hall to get Bryan's invitation rescinded. The mayor, who knew nothing about Wicca, was meanwhile finding out a little more about the religion.

The local newspapers picked up on the story. After the sensational events surrounding the Fort Hood Witches (about which more later), the press was very sensitive to Wiccan issues. The

Dallas Morning News and the *Fort Worth Star-Tel.*
lar were very fair in their reports.

Bryan and Maeven, accompanied by several sι
tended the city council meeting and sat quietly and
through the Reverend Britt's invocation. Then they left   ..am-
bers, intending to perform their own invocation outside, where
the reporters waited. As they left, Mayor Ron Kirk, incidentally
the city's first black mayor, expressed his regret and offered Lankford an apology, saying that there had been a disservice done and
that he'd like to reschedule. Later that day, a phone call set Bryan's
invocation for October 4.

Some things helped Bryan along. For one thing, he had a fair-
minded mayor and several council members on his side, notably
councilwoman Laura Miller, who is Jewish. "It's important to have
prayers from all kinds of people," she said. "I still flinch when
they end the prayers in the name of Jesus Christ, because that's
not all of our religion."

The day of Bryan's invocation, you would have thought it was
a paparazzi convention with all the cameras, lights, reporters, and
film crews. One protester from the crowd tried to stop the pro-
ceedings but was threatened with ejection by the mayor. Council
member Donna Blumer refused to bow her head, saying later, "I
wanted to make it very clear that their faith did not reflect my
faith."

But the invocation went beautifully, making history as the first
Dallas City Council invocation ever delivered by a Wiccan.

Afterward, Mayor Kirk stated, "The city council is not in the
business of choosing one faith over another. I was moved by the
invocation that was given today, as I have been before. An invocation is a *prayer,* not a manifesto."

Bryan showed a lot of the qualities and techniques that make for
a successful protest. He was willing to compromise. He took the
issue seriously, but didn't set himself up as a Wiccan Martyr. He
was positive and insistent about his rights without being confron-

.ational and obnoxious, and—most important—he *stayed focused on the issue at hand,* without muddying the waters by veering off into every Wiccan grievance since the dawn of time.*

And the Wiccans and Pagans who turned out to support him were serious, friendly, and informative when talking to the press. Almost all dressed in regular clothes, not costumes, and treated the incident not as a confrontation, but as an opportunity to support Wicca and one of their own. It illustrates a point that one robed Wiccan was singled out in some reports as eccentric or wacky-looking. The press *looks* for this stuff and it isn't complimentary to us.

A side note here: It didn't hurt that Bryan showed up for every meeting with the press and the city in a really great-looking Armani suit and a knockout tie. The guy knows how to work the crowd, for sure.

It's also interesting that the goals that Bryan and Maeven set for themselves involved the community as a whole: Wiccans, certainly, will benefit, but so will the school system and the local government.

While too much of Wiccan "activism" is actually aimed at "my coven, my group, my Trad," real and effective activism involves larger issues that benefit a wider segment of the world. As Maeven Eller said, "We're trying to build bridges between Witches and the community, and between faiths."

The Fracas at Fort Hood

Texas Wiccans will be the first to tell you that the Fort Hood demonstration was probably the best thing that ever happened to them, and they owe it all to some redneck preacher and to

---

*As a historical sidelight, it illustrates the point to note here that early efforts for women's suffrage failed miserably because the organizers insisted on tying the issue of women's right to vote to the temperance issue. The right to vote has zilch to do with drinking, unless you're attending the Republican or Democratic National Conventions and you're on an expense account.

Representative Bob Barr, a religious conservative from Georgia. In an effort to make Wicca look bad, Barr and friends only made themselves look silly and bigoted, while affording Wicca some very good press from newspapers that were appalled at the undignified antics of the religious right.

Fort Hood, Texas, is the nation's largest military base, with 340 square miles and forty-two thousand troops. The base has a lot of Pagans, and the Circles on the base are sponsored by the Sacred Well Congregation of San Antonio, on a nice campground operated by Fort Hood. The high priest of Sacred Well is a retired army major, David Oringderff; his wife, Tama, is the high priestess.

All was going quietly until the *Austin American-Statesman* ran an article on the Circles; the novelty value of Wiccans in the military sparked a lot of attention. Barr and fellow conservative Christian Strom Thurmond from South Carolina got wind of it and threw a hissy fit. (It's probably just a coincidence that Thurmond and Barr are Republicans, and George Bush the Second was making his bid to be president.) Barr tried to insert a provision in a military authorization bill that would have banned Wiccans from using base facilities or using candles supplied by the military, as is done for other chaplains. The bill died in committee.

All the publicity stirred up the Reverend Jack Harvey of Killeen, Texas, who saw his chance for some glory at the Wiccans' expense. As hard as it is to believe in this day and age, Harvey actually said that he heard that Wiccans eat babies and drink blood. He announced a Labor Day March Against Wickedness, and advised his congregation to carry handguns "in case those warlocks try to grab one of our kids." They showed up with signs saying things like GOD HATES WICCA and managed to look so intolerant that people in the entire state expressed distaste.

What Harvey mainly did was mobilize support for Wicca from the people around Fort Hood, especially real Christians, who were very embarrassed over Harvey's drama-queen tactics. Harvey's March Against Wickedness didn't come off very well; people in the community refused to support him, especially pastors and

Christians from other churches. According to the Reverend Gary Kindler of the First Methodist Church of Killeen, "People who are hypercritical to the point of paranoia do not represent mainline Christian thought or mainline churches in Killeen."*

Before we jump on "Christians" as across-the-board haters of Wicca, we should look at the particular Christians who are denouncing us. In almost every case, it's not the established Christian churches but the fringe-group evangelicals, "Bible believers," or fundamentalists out to make names for themselves or to make a political point. Most of these people don't like *anyone* who's not part of their particular cult, and they believe that most Christians are going to burn right along with us Witches. Yep, Lutherans, Episcopalians, Methodists, Mormons, and Wiccans are all going to be sharing a bathroom in hell. And don't even bring up the Catholics and Jews.

I found this out for myself when some "good Christians" were upset at our town for letting my coven hold our afternoon Beltane celebration in a local park. One of our public defenders was a Baptist minister who remembered the history of his own church, when Baptists were being shot at and lynched. He didn't agree with us or even like us, but he wasn't going to stand for any religious discrimination. And that was good enough for us.

How to Write Activist Letters

There's no denying that good, sensible letters can do a lot to advance the cause of Wicca. But a bad letter, ranting and raving and with terrible spelling, can set us back. During the 1980s, the Reverend Donald Wildmon terrorized the entertainment media by barraging them with letters, actually getting commercials and shows pulled off the air if they offended his right-wing religious

---

Fort Worth Star-Telegram, "Bothered and Bewildered: Wiccans at Hood Shrug Off Media Hubbub," by Barry Shlachter, August 7, 1999.

views. He didn't have a lot of members in his group, but the members he did have were willing to write letters all damn day long.

There's a great quote about how "anyone can control the media with ten little old ladies armed with ballpoint pens." I don't remember who said it, but it's true. It might have even been Donald Wildmon.

Here are some pointers on how to improve your letter-writing skills.

- Keep it short and to the point. The person you're writing to probably gets a lot of mail, and one of the last things he or she wants to deal with is complaint letters. Get your point across quickly—don't ramble on in the first or second paragraph before you get to the real purpose of the letter.
- Don't go on forever about the entire history of Wicca—just get to whatever it was that offended you, or that was wrong.
- Always make it clear that Wicca is a religion. Corporations are terrified of offending religious groups.
- Don't make threats—it sounds stupid. Don't say that a million Wiccans will never watch that TV show or buy that product again. You don't have the authority to speak for anyone but yourself, even if you're the head of a big Wiccan organization (if you are, just point out that your group has X number of members). But you have a perfect right to express your own feelings: Companies expect that for every one letter they get, there are many more people who feel as you do, but didn't write. That's one reason that many companies take well-written, sensible complaint letters seriously.
- Use your spell checker, or have a friend check over what you've written for grammar and spelling errors. Your letter won't be taken seriously if it sounds like it came from an illiterate fourteen-year-old.
- Make sure your facts are straight, and be specific. If you're complaining about a TV show, for instance, give the name of the show and the date, time, and station on which it aired. If

you're complaining about a magazine or newspaper article, you need the title of the piece and the date it ran. If you're complaining to a store about a product, include the name of the product and the manufacturer's name—and send a copy of your letter to the manufacturer, if possible.

- *Type the letter* or print it out from your word processing program on good paper, and include your return address on the letter, not just on the envelope.
- Sound professional, not obnoxious, and never use obscenity. That's guaranteed to get the letter tossed immediately, because it will look like a crank letter from a nutcase. Keep in mind that most things that you see as "an insult" were not meant to be insulting in the first place. You're going to have to assume that an insult was inadvertent: You might want to say, "You may not be aware of it, but . . ."
- What action do you want them to take? Make a suggestion as to how to fix the situation.
- Write directly to the person or institution, and send copies to whomever else should be interested. Try to get a specific name of the person to write to. If you're writing to a store, for instance, write to the manager, but send a copy to the CEO or other people who'd be directly interested and responsible.

Wiccan Antidiscrimination Organizations

Get two or three politically minded Wiccans together and they'll invariably start an antidiscrimination organization. This is a good thing: The more Wiccans engaged in supporting other Wiccans and improving the image of the religion, the better.

But make sure that the organization you're supporting or joining is an effective and active one.

If you're thinking of giving money or time to a group, you should do all you can to find out more about what it actually does, and don't fall for a famous name: Some groups that were very active in the past are now just coasting, or new people have taken over and may not be as effective as the old crew. Most Wiccan groups aren't scammers, they're just badly organized and ignorant of the law. They mean well, but it can be very easy for some charlatan to take over and scam *them*—and you—since the group's leaders can change frequently, sometimes according to whim or internal Witch Wars. You should never give your money to an organization unless you know how the money's being spent and what the group really does.

Ask to look at the financial statements. I asked several prominent groups about this, and got an answer from only one of them; it had forwarded the inquiry to the regional director. The complete answer was "We use the money to fight for the rights of Pagans." *That* was enlightening.

One organization required a membership fee up front, promising that your money would be put to good use and that you'd get a newsletter to keep you up on what issues the group was involved with. Ha. If you were *lucky,* you got a newsletter, because it only managed to put out a single issue in three years. And *that* was back in the 1980s. As far as a regular financial statement to be made available to the membership, you were going to be hardpressed to see one. I know. I asked, in person. *Nada.*

Here are some guidelines to make sure you're doing some social good—not helping someone get goodies.

- Ask about the organization's track record. What has it accomplished and how recently? How does it keep the members of the group informed of its activities?
- If the organization is a nonprofit, ask to see a financial statement. By law, nonprofits have to file IRS Form 990 every year, and they're required to share these forms with anyone who asks to see them, although they are allowed to charge a reasonable fee for sending the form to you or making a copy. Form 990 summarizes the organization's finances, lists the salaries of the highest-paid officials, lists the names of the

board members, notes "insider" transactions, and gives you a general overview of the organization.

- *Nonprofit* doesn't mean that the organization isn't allowed to make money: It just means that the money must be used for the stated purpose of the organization. On the state level, *nonprofit* is used to describe corporations that are organized to advance a public or community interest rather than for individual personal or financial gain.

- Nonprofits are asked by the state to provide a mission statement that tells what the organization is; a purpose statement that tells what the organization wants to accomplish or the problem it seeks to correct; a business statement that outlines the activities that will accomplish that purpose; and a value statement that specifies the basic beliefs that are shared by the organization's members. Ask to see these documents. (If you're thinking of forming a group, these are important statements for you to consider, too, and once you finalize them, they should be available in print or on your Web site.)

- How can you contribute? Money or efforts? You should ask yourself this question before you join. Many people join groups and then never do anything to support them.

- Read the group's printed materials or Web site carefully.

- If you're sending money, check the group's credentials. Call your state's attorney general's office and see if it has info on the group, or if there have been any complaints. Never give anyone cash—write a check or send a money order by mail. That will be your receipt in case you don't get another one.

- Be sure that you get what you're paying for: If you, as a member of an organization, are entitled to certain things, like a newsletter or a membership kit or a free e-mail address, you should get them in a reasonable amount of time. If you don't, that's a sign of some trouble.

Nonprofit organizations are not the same as tax-exempt organizations. For more information on tax-exempt groups, read on.

Becoming Legal: Wicca and Tax-Exempt Status

It's not so much the prospects of not having to pay taxes that makes 501(c)(3) status so desirable; it's the many benefits of becoming an organized religion.

Status 501(c)(3) is the IRS code for tax-exempt groups, including churches. Tax exempt status means that your nonprofit religious or secular organization doesn't pay income tax and other taxes. It also allows people to donate money to your organization and take the contribution off their own taxes. To get tax-exempt status, you have to apply to the IRS, which will then send you—surprise!—some forms to fill out.

If you incorporate as a religious organization, or a church, you can ordain ministers; conduct legal marriages, funerals, and prison religious counseling; get group health insurance for clergy; and buy tax-free land or buildings for church use. One of the most important benefits is that you can get liability insurance: something you'll definitely want if you're doing public Circles. More important, being a legal organization gives you more clout in discrimination cases.

Gavin and Yvonne Frost paved the way for the rest of us when they decided to get tax-exempt status for the Church and School of Wicca in North Carolina. It was a long nightmare of red tape and endless bureaucracy, but they finally succeeded in 1972. Theirs was the first Wiccan group to do so.

Doing business with the Internal Revenue Service still isn't easy, but it can be done, if you're not easily intimidated by paperwork. In fact, you might want to consult a good tax attorney, because you're sailing the tricky waters between the Charybdis of the U.S. government and the Scylla of state regulations.

If you haven't been scared off so far, here's a little more information:

The IRS, with typical governmental zeal, will ask you to fill out something called Schedule A of Form 1023. Get ready for writer's cramp. The IRS wants to know:

- A brief history of the development of your group, including the reasons for its formation. *This says "brief," so don't feel that you have to go into the Paleolithic roots of Pagan practice. Also, be specific about your particular group—not Wicca as a whole.*
- A copy of your written creed or faith. *The Wiccan Rede and the Threefold Law can help you here.*
- A description of your faith's formal code of doctrine and discipline for members. *For example, do you have a degreed training system?*
- A description of your form of worship. You must attach a schedule of worship services for the current year. *If you honor the eight Sabbats, you've got this one licked.*
- An explanation of how your group attracts new members. *This is tricky for us because we don't recruit or try to convert. But do explain that people come to us of their own accord.*
- Number of active members in your group and average attendance numbers for a worship service.
- Additional religious services, such as weddings, funerals, and baptisms, that your group conducts. *Baptisms?*
- If the group licenses ministers, the requirements for ministerial candidates.
- Number of hours and amount of compensation that minister and church officers devote to church work.

Some of these questions are deceptively simple. That's why it's best to have a tax lawyer look over your answers.

If you've come this far, you might also get an IRS group ruling, which allows a central organization to extend tax-exempt status to any subordinate group added to it. For instance if your Coven of the Silver Whatsis has tax-exempt status, you can get a "group extension letter" from the IRS so that any covens hiving off Silver Whatsis may also share that tax-exempt status. You can update the list of your hived-off groups once a year.

All this involves a lot of time and paperwork. This is why many

Wiccans have chosen the easiest route, which is to incorporate under the group exemption extended by the Universal Life Church in Modesto, California. For years, the ULC was the only way that Wiccans could become legal ministers, so we owe the group a debt of gratitude. The ULC is the original "mail-order ministry" that everyone jokes about, but to the founder, the Reverend Kirby Hensley, it was no joke: It was his life's work. Hensley believed that if you felt called to the ministry, then you should be ordained: It was between you and God (or the gods—Reverend Hensley never discriminated, and faith is a personal matter). The ULC has only one doctrine: Do That Which Is Right. Hensley said, "We must teach that this planet, Earth, belongs to us, all people, and that we must set up a kingdom of peace, joy and love." I know very few Wiccans who'd argue with this.

According to the Reverend Hensley, "I started out as a Baptist, but I guess I was too emotional for the Baptists." He tried several other groups, including some "I Am" groups and spiritualists. Then in 1957, disillusioned with the commercialism of religion, he broke away from *all* groups. He started an independent church in his garage in Modesto, putting up a sign that simply said, CHURCH. After a while, he "got tired of teaching the 'death' message" and added the word *Life* to the church. In 1962, the Life Church incorporated, so he added *Universal* to the name, becoming the Universal Life Church.

His plan was to spread faith rather than religion: "The vision is to release people from religious bondage," he said. "Most churches today keep you in bondage, so they can rob you financially." Hey, *he* said it, I'm just quoting it.

To be ordained as a minister in the Universal Life Church gives you legal status in all fifty states. You can perform legal marriages and all the rest. All you need to do is write the Universal Life Church and say that you want to be ordained, and you'll get a ministerial card and a nice certificate. You'll also get materials from the ULC, including a list of each state's requirements for performing marriages. (It varies from state to state, so this info is good to know. If you need anything besides your credentials, the ULC will provide it for you.) It doesn't cost anything, but most people kick in some bucks as a donation. Be aware that simply being ordained does not confer tax-exempt status. For that, you need to incorporate as a congregation of the Universal Life Church. Since this involves paperwork and record keeping, the ULC asks a thirty-five-dollar donation when you fill out the paperwork, and a five-dollar donation per month to keep the required quarterly reports. This makes your coven a legal, tax-exempt church under IRS rules. You can still use your coven name, but must append *Universal Life Church* onto it, such as Coven of the Silver Whatsis, a Universal Life Church. The good thing about the ULC is that it has long ago met all the IRS requirements, and has been in existence just about as long as Gardnerian Wicca. You can contact the ULC at 601 Third Street, Modesto, CA 95351.

Of course, some Wiccan and Pagans organizations have bitten the red-tape bullet and acquired tax-exempt status. They also can ordain legal ministers. Some have also acquired the group extension, among them the Welsh group Y Tylwyth Teg, the Church of Wicca, Covenant of the Goddess, the Aquarian Tabernacle Church, and the Church of All Worlds.

The Big Drawback to Tax-Exempt Status

If your group is politically active, you might have to give that up if you want to keep your tax exemption. The government rules on this are very clear. If a substantial part of the activities of your organization consists of attempting to influence legislation, you can kiss that tax-exempt status good-bye. This means you can *forget* that letter-writing campaign to Congress for religious rights. "Attempting to influence legislation" is not illegal: It's a time-honored Washington tradition, and lobbyists make big bucks doing it. But your group isn't allowed to spend its money this way if it's tax exempt. You're going to have to decide if the tax-exempt status is worth the trade-off of not having a public voice in local, state, and federal government.

Influencing legislation consists of:

Grassroots lobbying. *Any attempt to influence any legislation through an effort to affect the opinions of the general public or any segment thereof.* Don't even think about circulating a petition or holding a press conference to get the state to repeal a repressive law.

Direct lobbying. *Any attempt to influence any legislation through communication with any member or employee of a legislative body or with any government official or employee who may participate in the formulation of legislation.* Thinking of getting your entire group to write to their representatives to oppose a certain House bill? Think again.

There are some things you *can* still do without endangering your 501(c)(3) status. *Warning: Governmental language ahead: may be too strong for sensitive readers.*

- Making available the results of nonpartisan analysis, study, or research.
- Examining and discussing broad social, economic, and similar problems.
- Providing technical advice or assistance (where the advice would otherwise constitute the influencing of legislation) to a governmental body or to a committee or other subdivision in response to a written request by that body or subdivision. In other words, if the House Committee on Pagans in the Military asks you for advice, you're allowed to give it to them.
- Appearing before, or communicating with, any legislative body about a possible decision of that body that might affect the existence of your organization, its powers and duties, its tax-exempt status, or the deduction of contributions to your group.
- Communicating with a government official or employee, as long as you're not trying to influence legislation.

- Communicating with the members of your group to discuss upcoming legislation that might affect the group—but you can't urge them to influence legislation, or encourage them to get nonmembers to try to influence legislation.

Quiet Activism: Working on Your Own

What if you're not in a coven, haven't joined a group, or can't possibly "come out" as a Wiccan or Pagan, but you still want to do something to advance the cause of your religion? Don't worry—there are plenty of things you can do! And here are a couple of them, courtesy of Cassius Julianus and The Julian Society.*

"Personals" Ads

If you look in the personals section of your local newspaper, you will see a really ingenious thing. Catholics take out ads to "Saint Jude" in thanks for some personal miracle that has happened. This short ad accomplishes three things:

1. It is a public admission of faith on the part of the person taking the ad.
2. It publicly states belief that this religion has produced results.
3. It gets the name of the saint out there.

Placing ads like these is cheap, perhaps three or four dollars. There is no reason that this technique cannot be used to further pantheist ends. The next time a ritual has worked for you, take an ad! "Thanks to the Goddess Isis [or whomever you work with] for prayers answered" can be a real eye-opener for all those scanning the ads section. Other "contact" ads can be taken as well . . . "Pagan looking for pen pals of like mind" along with a post office box address can lead to some interesting contacts.

*Cassius Julianus, *50 Things You Can Do to Advance Pagan Religion*, Wells, ME., The Julian Society, 1997.

Proselytize . . . gently

Pagans are not known for working to convert people. It is always best to tolerate other views, rather than to actively harass people to change their minds. Still, there are times when someone is looking for direction and can use positive help. If, at the right time, you can recommend a book or introduce others to Paganism, you are simply giving them new information so that they can make their own positive choice. Not everyone finds the path alone. If other religions can spend millions yearly to convert people, the least any of us can do is stand ready for when we may be needed. If it seems to you that you someone you know might be looking for the Pagan path, point the way. That person will either take it or not, depending upon his or her own inner needs. At least you will have done what you could.

10

You'll Never Cast a Spell in This Town Again

WITCH WARS, SCAMS, SECRETS, AND LIES, AND OTHER NASTY HABITS

Okay, I'm giving you the warning about this chapter right up front.

It's not exactly Paganly Correct, and it's gossipy. In fact, there are a lot of really unpleasant things here, true stories that don't show Wiccans and Pagans in the best light. So if you don't like this sort of thing, skip this chapter. No kidding: It will only upset you, and then you'll be writing me indignant letters—and then I'll get pissed off and we'll both have ulcers.

But you know and I know that stuff like this goes on, for whatever reason. If you're just starting out in Wicca, you might as well face it now so that you can avoid it later. If you've been in the Wiccan and Pagan communities for a while, I'll bet that you have stories that will make these look like Free Prozac Day at the local theme park. The point of recounting these lurid tales is that we need to start watching what we do—watching *our own* actions. There's probably not one of us who hasn't been drawn into, or even initiated, some ugly Witch Wars or power struggles, and most of us deeply regret it later. Unfortunately, some of us go right on repeating the experience. Who knows why? Because of the sense of drama and importance it brings into our lives? Because dealing with someone who's acting like an idiot (in our opinion, anyway) makes us feel better about ourselves? Take it up with your therapist, because I certainly don't have a clue why it happens. All I know is that it does. Frequently.

I can tell you one cause of Witch Wars, and this I know because I was directly involved. It was absolutely one of the worst experiences of my life, and finally resulted in one of those messages from the gods that change your attitude and your life. Well, it wasn't so much a *message* as a hard whack upside the head. And if you priestesses and priests take anything away from this book, please take my advice on this one: *If you're a high priestess or priest, do not involve your coven in your own personal likes and dislikes about others and the way they practice.* You're not advancing the cause of religion; you're teaching intolerance.

To be perfectly honest, I don't even remember all the details because it went on for a while and became fairly confusing—and I think I've blanked it out from embarrassment—but the gist of it is this. I had formed my first coven, a teaching coven, and we were attracting a lot of people brand new to Wicca. I was really determined to give them the best possible instruction, since they would be expected to form covens of their own. My high priest and I had pretty much determined that we'd have a "core" coven, with a lot of transient students practicing with us until they were initiated and felt confident to proceed on their own.

The instruction they were getting was pretty good, actually, and I guess it stuck, because a lot of them are still with it, a lot *have* formed their own groups, and I hear from many of them. Note here that I didn't say I hear from *all* of them. That's significant.

Because after they were trained and practicing with the core group, I sure made it hard on them. Frankly, I was a religious fanatic, a fundamentalist Wiccan. I was filled with a lot of intolerance for another couple of groups that I felt were making the religion look bad. I wanted to make sure that "my babies" weren't contaminated by those people, who seemed to treat the religion with irreverence and were just "not serious." The weird part was that I actually liked most people in those groups, having worked with them before and having had a lot of fun, but when I became a priestess I just felt that they were a bad influence, and bad-mouthed them over every little thing.

Can you get more smug and self-righteous than that? And what was all that overprotective crapola? My students were not kids, they were intelligent adults and quite capable of making their own decisions and value judgments. I'm amazed they weren't turned off Wicca for life.

So I'm telling all of you who teach and who have people for whom you are responsible: Check your own attitude at the door, and stay off your high horse. Concentrate your energies on your teaching.

We like to say that Wicca is nonjudgmental, but that only goes so far. Having no prejudices about race, gender, sexual preference, or other externals does *not* make us nonjudgmental. The harshest critics of Wiccans are other Wiccans, especially if we're doing it in the name of religious sanctity. I mean, I'm writing this and you're reading it, so what's up with *that?* The trick is to keep the criticism constructive. You can give your opinion—I'm certainly giving mine—but don't expect others to change just because you say so. Free will, ain't it a bitch?

Mainly, Witch Wars happen because some of us are convinced that how we're practicing Wicca is right and what others are doing or practicing is wrong: *We're* upstanding Wiccans following the path of righteousness, and *those* people are nasty warlocks, a disgrace to the religion. Because Wicca is so flexible and the doctrine so open to interpretation, it's easy to tell ourselves that a difference of opinion is grounds for war. And frankly, Wiccans, Witches, and Pagans are often drama queens, the men as bad as the women. I've never met one who isn't, and I've met a whole lot of us, including the Big Name Pagans. That's not necessarily a bad thing: It's what makes us interesting. But carried to extremes, it can make our lives and the lives of people around us a misery, and can make Wicca look bad if the high drama goes public.

Witch Wars are always going to happen. And if you think it only happens in Wicca, you might ask yourself where all those Protestants came from.

But at least we can stop ourselves from broadcasting it all over the place in the mainstream press. Every catfight between two Witches that gets covered in the papers by an amused press on a slow news day makes us look flat-out ludicrous.

This isn't to say that if we have a problem with another Wiccan, we can't try to do something about it. It isn't to say that we can't go to court or call the cops if we've had a real problem, or notify other Wiccans and Pagans if someone's ripping people off or hurting others. But let's keep the dirty undies in the family. Quit running to the media for every little thing, especially if you don't know the whole story. And if the press does get wind of a matter of public record, remember those two immortal and useful words: *No comment.*

If you're not directly involved in a Witch War or other unpleasantness, *stay out of it!* No kidding. Keep your head down and cover your jewels. For one thing, you probably don't know all the details, or you're hearing only one version. I'm not going to tell you to stay off the phone with your friends to rehash the gossip—get real; I've never known a Wiccan anywhere, no matter how pious, to pass up a good dish-the-dirt session. But avoid getting actively involved. And *especially* avoid making the situation worse.

So, you've had the warning. Those with strong stomachs can read on.

More Persecuted Than Thou

We all know that discrimination exists. But is it as widespread as some Wiccans make it out to be? And are some of us actually courting disaster? Do we see fire where there's barely any smoke?

Some Wiccans don't wait to be marginalized by society: They

jump right in there and do it themselves. They almost guarantee discrimination, or—as they prefer to call it, because it's more dramatic—persecution.

When I was working with an antidiscrimination group, we took lots of calls from people who claimed they'd been ostracized just because they were Wiccans. When we dug a little deeper, it sometimes turned out that these people were asking for trouble from the beginning. They used no common sense whatsoever. They'd go to job interviews at conservative companies decked in their trashiest Goth gear and biggest pentagrams. When dealing with people who were not Wiccan or Pagan, they had an attitude. When they didn't get what they wanted or weren't treated as they thought they *should* be treated, they screamed "discrimination."

This last one really hit home with me. One night I went to dinner with some friends and some new acquaintances, all Pagans. The restaurant was crowded and obviously short of help, so it was a while before we got menus. While we waited, some members of the group were getting very snippy. They decided that "the Christians" were getting served ahead of us and that we were being ignored because we were Pagans. Unfortunately, they wanted everyone in the place to overhear them as they started going on about discrimination. The rest of us were looking for a quick route out of the restaurant, preferably by ducking under the tables toward the door. Don't ask me how they arrived at the conclusion that everyone else in the place was Christian. I didn't notice anybody wearing a sign that said, ASK ME ABOUT JESUS or selling the *Watchtower*. And I guess the help was supposed to know that we were Pagans and Wiccans because some of us were wearing pentacles the size of Detroit.*

Not only was it embarrassing, it was stupid. These people wanted everyone around them to know that they were special.

---

*Good rule to remember: Not everybody knows what the pentagram means. If you're using it as an attention-getting device, you'll do better with a big sign that says I'M A WITCH!

And they couldn't wait to tell others how they were victims of discrimination.

This kind of behavior isn't limited to Pagans: You see it a lot among customers in trendy restaurants who want to impress people with how powerful they are. Obviously, the waitstaff is just too dumb to realize that Masters of the Universe have come to dine, so a little obnoxious bitching and moaning, followed by sending back the food before it's even tasted and rejecting the wine, gets the message across.

The message is: "Hiya! I'm an asshole!" Note: people who are nice to you but rude to the help are actually ill-bred sleazeballs.

Several Witches here in Salem make it a practice to visit stores during October and complain loudly about the green-faced witches on the Halloween decorations. Like it's some big surprise to see this stuff. If the Witches are so offended, you'd think a quiet word with the manager would be the first step, but I suppose they figure: Hey, why bother with that when you can issue an outraged press release and notify all the Wiccan Web sites? That way, you can draw lots of attention to yourself and give the impression that you're a "freedom fighter" into the bargain!

One of the "freedom fighters" got very belligerent with the manager of a local restaurant about his Halloween decorations. (Damn, doesn't *anyone* want to enjoy a peaceful meal around here?) The manager said he'd change whatever offended her, but the Witch was on a roll and threatened, "I can have a hundred Witches picketing this place by tomorrow!" *Woooooo* . . . what awesome power! And you know . . . that was what it was all about in the first place. The phrase wasn't even original: She'd heard a Big Name Pagan use it in just about the same context.

When I saw the manager a few days later, he was still upset, especially since local Witches had been dining at his place for years and were always treated well. Some of the waitstaff were Pagan. He couldn't understand what had set the woman off. I knew, but didn't tell him: The woman had just been made "director" of one of our many local antidiscrimination groups and wanted to throw her weight around to establish herself as a power to be reckoned with.

And this silliness isn't limited to American Witches. As of this writing, there are Witches in the United Kingdom making a big noise in the press about the Harry Potter movie. They're very concerned about Harry riding his broom with the bristles in the back: apparently not the historically accurate position. What's even worse is that they're serious. I'm not sure about Britain, but here in the United States brooms don't fly. Oh, I guess you could jump off a roof, but it would be a very short flight with a disappointing landing. And here I thought the Brits were more sensible than us—you know, the home of Gerald Gardner and all that. Sounds more like someone's trying to make himself a Big Name Pagan by piggybacking on the Harry Potter bandwagon.

What these people are doing is using Wicca to make themselves look important. Worse, they demean and trivialize the victims of real discrimination. Some Witches, especially out there in small or Bible Belt towns, are losing their homes, their jobs, their supposed friends, and their kids, and here are these pseudo-activists complaining about movies and green-faced Halloween cartoons. Talk about a nonissue. If they've got so much time and so much indignation, why can't they find a serious cause to work for? Voter registration among Witches is very low, so why aren't they getting out to vote? Why aren't they joining with groups like People for the American Way, a group that watchdogs the religious right? How come they're not working with the local shelter for abused women, escorting them to court so they'll have some emotional support?

It doesn't help that some of these indignant Witches who are so terribly concerned about the image of Wicca look like they just stepped out of a comic book themselves. Many are loud, rude, and crude. And lest you think you know who I'm talking about, let me be quick to say that there are many, many of them, all over the country. Idiocy knows no geographical boundaries.

Well . . . okay, maybe in parts of Dade County.

The Famous Victim Syndrome:
Be Careful What You Wish For

Why would anyone actually *want* to be the victim of discrimination?

After several high-profile cases of actual discrimination, some Witches or Wiccans noticed that they could get their names known and—as an added bonus—make out financially if they let it be known that they were being "persecuted." There would be editorials in the Pagan press, sympathy from Wiccans and Pagans all over the country, and big-time fund-raising efforts for a defense fund.

Some of them didn't care about the money, but they desperately wanted the attention and the sympathy.

It isn't only the bogus victims who are feeding this sort of nonsense: Many Wiccan organizations and covens either are taken in by the scam, or don't investigate too closely, especially if it's a high-profile case. Let's be charitable and say they're being taken in.

You wanna hear an extreme story? This one's a doozy.

One supposed victim managed to hoodwink several local Witches, a couple of antidiscrimination groups, several shop owners who organized fund-raisers, and the operators of a Wiccan Web site. As we'll see, however, he didn't manage it alone.

Lord Noname's* story was very close to that of the famous Iron Oak case, in which Wiccans won a long, hard battle over home worship. Lord Noname said that he was being discriminated against because he was holding religious services at home. His town had an ordinance against this. He claimed that no other religious groups were being held to the ordinance. The town said that this wasn't true; the ordinance applied to everyone. The story kept getting more pitiful and more dramatic as the months passed, as

---

*You bet I'm changing the names here. I'm not giving these people any more publicity. Except for Laurie Cabot, who's famous anyway.

he claimed that his home was being vandalized and his family terrorized.

The curious part of this is that he had come to several Wiccan groups months before and asked for help. Our group was one of them. Some of us investigated and found that his story wasn't without holes: for instance, the zoning laws were not being selectively enforced, and he *was* in violation. He also talked about openly defying the town government by going to the press and goading them to take action. We advised him to forget the groups, forget the press, get a lawyer, and keep it low-key while he was trying to work it out with the town council. Any publicity at that point was only going to make it impossible to negotiate.

But something just seemed fishy. He talked a lot about getting Laurie Cabot, the most famous Witch in Massachusetts, to "take his case," and he wanted us to introduce him to her. If we couldn't do that, could we introduce him to other groups?

Noname said that he had contacted Cabot's group, the Witches' League for Public Awareness, and hadn't heard from them. (The WLPA was in the middle of reorganizing at that time.) When he couldn't get Cabot's attention, he turned to other groups to garner publicity. He contacted Witches Against Religious Discrimination and the Witches Anti-Defamation League in both Massachusetts and—for some reason—Connecticut, both of which promised support. Why would they not? This sounded like the real thing, and they took him at his word. The Connecticut Wiccan and Pagan Network was stretched pretty thin right about then, having become involved with a serious local case in its own state, but it generously agreed to include him in a fund-raiser being organized for its own case.

After trying more groups, Noname ended up under the direction of Lady PoohBah, the vociferous priestess of a coven near Boston and an old hand at recognizing a media opportunity. Lady PoohBah put the publicity machine in high gear. Internet newsgroup posts and Wiccan Web sites were carrying the story. Soon, Noname's tales of abuse from the town fathers and terrorism by the local people were getting more and more horrendous. There were regular bulletins from PoohBah about the progress of the case. The victim finally got a lawyer. PoohBah contacted store owners and covens to hold fund-raisers and had them put collection jars in the shops for the defense fund.

Amid all the publicity, Noname was finally introduced to Cabot, and the WLPA offered its support. He was initiated into the Cabot Tradition, taking the Cabot name and wearing the Cabot plaid robes. At last, he had gotten what he wanted.

It was going to cost him. Cabot and PoohBah had a history, and it wasn't a friendly one.

Suddenly things got very, very complicated, with PoohBah insisting that Noname's lawyer include her in the preparations for trial, and demanding to see all the related legal papers, something that the lawyer refused to comply with. The lawyer complained of being harassed by phone calls from PoohBah, who said that unless *she* vouched for Noname in court, affirming that he was an initiated Witch and a legal minister, they could kiss their case goodbye. If he wasn't a Witch and a minister, then it wasn't a religious discrimination case.

Then, everything changed.

The story started circulating that Lord Noname was no victim at all, but a scam artist instead. There were terrible rumors going around about his personal behavior, his habits, and his marriage. People claimed they'd been taken in. Many were hurt and angry, and rightfully so: They'd tried to do the right thing, helping one of their own, and look how they were suckered.

Suddenly, he was summoned before a "Council of Elders" hastily organized from among his former supporters and others by PoohBah, to "answer charges for crimes against the Wiccan Rede." He was told to bring his lawyer and legal papers with him.

At that point, unfortunately, he called me. *Oh, joy.* I hadn't heard much from this character in weeks, except for his calling to tell me about his shiny new initiation, and from his lawyer calling to ask about PoohBah's authenticity as a "Wiccan Leader," but I had already heard plenty from the supporters and organizers of the defense funds, especially after they'd been taken in. Now he was in a panic, spilling out the entire history of the case, which I'd already watched unfolding. You know: Like watching a train wreck? Specifically, he wanted to know what to do about the Council of Elders: Should he answer their summons? Should he bring his lawyer? He had promised to take his family out of town that weekend to escape some of the pressure, but he said that the Council of Elders insisted he appear or suffer the consequences. (He didn't say what those consequences were, but I'm sure an apology was the least of it.)

"What should I do?" he wailed.

"Forget it," I told him. *Take your family on vacation, get some sleep, think about what an asshole you've been.* I didn't say, *I told you so,* but I really, really wanted to.

"But they say I *have* to show up."

"Yeah? What part of the Constitution says that?" *Please, get off the phone and go have a beer. Have several.* "Exactly what are they going to do to you if you don't show up? Look, pal, you're going to be guilty no matter what. If you think this is anything except a kangaroo court, you're dreaming. Save your energy and your lawyer's hourly fees for your *real* court case."

He hung up, still worried, but I understand he didn't attend the Council of Elders court, preferring to be with his wife and child. So the Inquisi . . . I mean, Council of Elders, announced that Lord Noname didn't show up and was therefore guilty of whatever it was they were charging him with.

Not that this guy was an innocent or any less of a jerk. He may have had a perfectly good case against the town, but he blew it by not following standard legal procedure and by wanting to present himself to the Pagan community as a Famous Victim, riding the publicity bandwagon.

And some of the organizations that were taken in were supposed to be experienced in matters of discrimination cases: After all, that's why those groups were formed. It's very simple for a group to check on the claims of discrimination victims: What happened, what are the local or state laws and ordinances, was there a violation, was there a police report, is there a court case pending, who is the victim's lawyer? The lawyer is not required, or even allowed, to release privileged information between lawyer and client, but in a discrimination case many lawyers are willing to work with competent antidefamation groups, within reason. And the groups *must* defer to the lawyer's experience and instructions.

The shop owners who took part in fund-raisers and kept collection jars in their shops told me that they did so because they were assured by PoohBah that it was a legitimate case, and because it was getting a lot of publicity. She was their friend; they trusted her judgment.

What happened to the money? I'm assuming, with no evidence but with eternal hope, that it went to defray lawyer's fees.

Incidentally, the Council of Elders is still around, still summoning people to answer for "crimes against the Rede," and still recruiting members by playing on the Wiccan's greatest weak spot: ego. No kidding, it's like Kryptonite is to Superman. Some people can't resist being told, "We want you to join us because you're a respected leader of the Pagan community," especially if it's accompanied by the assurance that you'll be Serving the Goddess by ridding Wicca of "charlatans" (their term) who give us a bad name and tarnish the image of the religion.

As I recall, this was frighteningly similar to the reasoning held by those righteous people dedicated to ridding the community of witches or purging the country of Commies.

The members of the council are encouraged to name offenders and turn in the guilty parties. People have been summoned for some really insignificant things. What amazes me is that some of them actually show up.

Plus, you've got to wonder about Lady PoohBah's sincerity here. Shortly after the Lord Noname debacle, she appeared in full color in the local trashy tabloid newspaper, dressed in complete Disney

Witch regalia, berating Laurie Cabot in the most insulting terms for dressing the way she does, and accusing Cabot of using Witchcraft for publicity reasons. Really improved the public perception of Witches. Incidentally, the story was headlined, BROOM SCHTICK. Oy.

When one potential Council of Elders member told me she was asked to join and I asked why on earth she'd even consider it, she said, "Well, *somebody's* got to set some standards." Goddess help us all if those standards turn out to be set by power-mongers and publicity hounds.

The lesson here, folks, is to make sure of the causes you support. Don't buy into something just because it's backed by some Big Name Pagan or organization. Check them out for yourself, especially if it involves money. *Especially* if you heard about it on the Internet, where there's a new scam every day and new suckers who fall for it. I actually read an Internet message from someone who complained that he lost money and *then* said, "Well, I thought it was probably a scam, but I sent them money anyway because you never know."

The problem with the Wiccan and Pagan communities is that they're way too gullible, and scammers know that claiming "discrimination" or "persecution" is the fastest way to big bucks.

Part of this gullibility is the assumption that Wiccans and Pagans are somehow above bad behavior. I wish I had a dollar for every time I heard of someone doing something reprehensible, and bystanding Wiccans chimed in with, "Oh, no . . . s/he wouldn't do anything like that! S/he's *Pagan!*" Or taking expensive athames or other magical objects to a Wiccan gathering with hundreds of people, then when the object goes missing, they're mystified. "But everyone here is *Pagan!*"

Ya wonder how some people manage to get themselves dressed without help.

The Victim Mentality

Some people just love abuse. Make-believe abuse, actually. They court it like Romeo courted Juliet and then they whine endlessly and loudly about how abused they are *just because they're Pagan*.

Most of these types have been professional victims all their lives, and Wicca just gives them a new context for it.

They're living a self-fulfilling prophecy. They come into Wicca because they didn't get enough abuse from the Catholic Church (although they complain about how terrible the nuns were in Catholic school) or from their straitlaced Baptist families or from their godless atheist parents or from the perps of whatever background they profess.

They usually start out in a very traditional Gardnerian coven, then leave and complain about how strict and structured it was, and how they weren't allowed to exercise their "natural" magical abilities because of the degree system. They go from coven to coven, group to group, and bitch about every one of them, not understanding that their complaints say much more about them than about the groups. They expect the coven to concern itself with their personal issues, and get offended if the group refuses.

They're very much in your face, decking themselves out in jewelry by the pound, black robes or Goth gear and makeup, gaudy tattoos in obvious places and a chip on the shoulder that could support Ah-nold Schwarzenegger, if he put on a few pounds. Their entire purpose is to shock, which is why they joined "the Craft," as they insist on calling it (since they're certainly not seriously interested in *religion*), in the first place. They show up for job interviews dressed like this, a walking, talking, sneering middle finger, clearly signaling that if you hire them, get ready for some serious attitude. When they don't get the job, they tell everyone that it was because they're being persecuted.

If they're invited to a family Thanksgiving or Christmas party, they make sure that no one leaves unoffended, lecturing about persecution by Christians and "the Burning Times" to people who have no idea what they're going on about.

Everything offends them; they can find an insult in the mildest remark or even a look. Forget about personal responsibility for your own actions: these folks don't want to hear it.

I'll betcha they even pick the green-faced M&Ms out of the bag.

Occult Slavery

Why is it that many intelligent people suddenly become four-year-olds when they decide to learn Wicca?

Let's say you're a competent professional, good at your job and managing your hectic life pretty well. You make important decisions, you stay more or less organized, you have a position for which you take responsibility, and you work hard.

Then one day you decide you'd like to learn Wicca, and three months later you're down on your knees scrubbing some high priestess's bathroom floor because she's told you that you have to "suffer to learn." And you're just blissfully happy about it. Oh, sometimes that nagging little voice in the back of your head pops up and says, *What the* hell *do you think you're doing?* but you tell yourself that's just your old life talking. Besides, there are all these other "newbies" doing errands for the high priestess—you're part of a community! No, a *family!*

What's wrong with this picture?

I'll tell ya what's wrong with it. (You knew that I would.) The main thing that's wrong is that this is *not* a legitimate part of Wicca. The second thing is that people assume (or they're told) that becoming a Wiccan means that you have to give up or modify your "old life"; that all the principles you formerly held no longer apply. The third thing is that you shouldn't be scrubbing anyone's bathroom floor unless (1) it's a good friend's bathroom and she's got the flu so bad that she's unable to move, and she'd do the same for you, or (2) you're a professional cleaner and you're getting paid for the job.

How do sane, grown-up people get rooked into giving their lives—and sometimes a great deal of their money—over to some self-styled "Elder of the Craft," usually getting nothing of sub-stance in return? Why do they put up with being reduced to the status of a child or a servant?

For the answer, we have to start with the attitude of most new-comers. Many of them feel that there are True Secrets that can only be taught by an Enlightened Elder. In this country, we're trained to think that knowledge is something that can be bought, or that can be attained in a semester's time if you study the books, follow the curriculum, and pass the exam. To make it worse, Wicca has the reputation of being "occult" in the sense that there are great secrets to be learned, only the initiated can teach them, and only old souls can learn them. It isn't uncommon to feel that, in approaching Wicca, we're approaching new territory to which there is no map, and everything depends on the expertise of the guide, like following a Sherpa up a mountain in a snowstorm.

People brought up in the traditions of mainstream religions are also conditioned to think that only priests or ministers can inter-pret spiritual matters. *They'll* be the ones to tell you what the Word o' God is, thank you very much, because they have a degree from divinity school or have been anointed by some earthly au-thority to prove that they've got a direct pipeline to the Big Guy. That's why people send money to Big-Haired Televangelists to ask them to pray for 'em: You could pray yourself, but the TV boys have influence! Or that's what people have been made to believe, anyway. And as for the pope . . . *fugeddaboudit!* The guy's sup-posed to be the direct spiritual descendant of Saint Peter himself, which is why he gets to wear the flashy jewelry and the big hat. Not to mention that his decisions are infallible, based as they are on a couple of thousand years of rock-solid dogma.

If you went to Sunday school, you've got even more condition-ing to overcome: You were taught to sit still and listen to the teacher, and only acceptable questions were answered. (*Hint:* "Was there really a Jesus?" was something only a foul heretic—or a future Jesuit—would think to ask in the first place, indicating poor religious training at home.) Little Catholic kids learned the Catechism, and that was supposed to answer all those tough questions. If it wasn't in the Catechism, you didn't need to know it. You aren't taught to think: You're taught to learn by rote. The church isn't going to let some ten-year-old kid question two thousand years of doctrine. No matter what you want to know, there's a canned answer for it.

If you were a girl, you really came in for the brainwashing. Girls grew up to know their place in the church, and that place was in the Altar Society or the Protestant equivalent, polishing the silver candlesticks, washing and ironing the altar linen, and waxing the pews. What a deal! Why hire a cleaning service, when you've got an entire legion of little old ladies panting to serve God by scrubbing the church windows?

Jewish folks had it a little better. Arguing over the Talmud is a fine art among Jews, and is thought to be the best way to learn it. Of course, for thousands of years, you had to be a guy to get in on the sanctified fun.

If you stuck to all this, you would attain Ultimate Enlightenment. The glitch was you had to die first, but no system is perfect.

No matter how restrictive you feel that your former religion was, you'll probably admit that the formalized structure could be comforting. People often find it simpler to live by a set of rules without questioning them. And some religions count on this quality among their faithful to retain their strength.

People approaching Wicca for the first time bring a lot of old-time religious baggage with them. Plus, it's not a matter of just marching up to the parish priest or the rabbi and saying you want to convert; or standing up at Wednesday Prayer Meeting, tearfully recounting your evil life and accepting Jesus as your personal savior. (I was always amused and alarmed when I saw little kids do this. What kind of sins could they have possibly committed in their first six or eight years? Snatching their sister's Barbie outfits?

If little kids are sinning, I'll bet Barbie has *some* part in it, the materialistic Jezebel.)

Despite our public attitudes against "religious authorities" or "organized religion," Wiccans at first feel uncomfortable with the concept of spirituality coming completely from within the self in conjunction with the gods, and are eager to find the ideal teacher, the perfect course of study, the right book, that will give us the approved and genuine version of Wicca. And this makes some people ripe for manipulation by a charismatic personality or an overblown ego.

And so, carrying a load of preconceived ideas and conditioning, many otherwise sensible people willingly hand their lives over to an opportunist.

How do you avoid this? Let's play a quick game of Spot the Phony! You know you're probably being taken for a ride if any of these things occur.

You're asked to run a lot of personal errands or do personal chores for the high priest or priestess, and your personal life is supposed to take a backseat to the coven. Running personal errands is something you should never have to do, unless you volunteer. Now, having said that, I know that there are times when the coven has some big project going on—a gathering or some special event—and running around getting things organized is a part of getting it done. If your HP or HPs is hosting the event, it's only courtesy that the coven members offer to pitch in and help. And if everyone's helping, you shouldn't be standing around sucking your thumb. But if the high priest isn't getting his own hands dirty, and you never see the high priestess doing any gruntwork like everyone else, then somebody's just a *li-i-i-ttle* too full of him- or herself.

If the coven has something planned, and you opt out to spend time with your family or a previous commitment, you should not be made to feel guilty about it. The coven exists the same way a church exists: as a framework for worship. It facilitates the worship of the gods by organizing rituals, but they are by no means the only way to communicate with the deities. Wiccans, like members of other religions, like to observe the holidays together. But it doesn't make you less of a Wiccan if you miss a few meetings, or even a few Sabbats.

Some covens feel that they need a lot of people present in order to do magical workings. This is not true. I've seen big Circles that generated about as much magic as a rerun of *Gilligan's Island.* Only not as funny. And I've seen groups of two or three produce enough power to knock your socks off. Magic and spirituality is not and will never be about numbers.

Covens that make the members feel bad about not showing up for every activity remind me of those Southern Baptist churches that used to send little cards around to anyone who wasn't in church on Sunday. The cards said, "We missed you" and went on to lay down the guilt, assuming that if you weren't sick, you were just plain damned for obviously screwing around on Sunday when you should have been kicking in your share of the tithe.

You're told that you have to "earn" an initiation by doing the bidding of the priest or priestess. An initiation isn't "earned." Rather, the knowledge is attained. And it's attained by study and by personal insight given to you by the gods. An ethical HP or HPs will initiate you into a specific coven or Tradition if he or she feels you're serious about Wicca, that you've been willing to put in the necessary study/work, and that you've demonstrated that you know the rituals and philosophy of that specific coven or Trad. But the real aim of training is to be initiated, and it is the duty of the priest or priestess to take on this responsibility. If the HP or HPs doesn't feel you're ready, you should be given clear reasons that have to do with spiritual matters. As a rule, if you're associating with a coven or Trad that has people who have been waiting years for a First Degree initiation, your warning bells should ring.

You're required to change your name to that of the high priestess or priest, or incorporate that name into your own. Wiccans usually select a "Wiccan name" when they come into the religion, an element imported from ceremonial magic and other occult groups. It's supposed to be a name with strong personal meaning for you. But if someone *requires* you to take a certain name, watch out, because you may be dealing with a cult of personality. The rationale behind this might be explained away with the "we're all a family" excuse, but in reality, be wary of anyone who insists that you forsake your own name or the name that you choose. This is a hallmark of many cults, and is a depersonalization method. And before you jump to any conclusions, I'm not saying that all groups that do this are dangerous cults. But it *is* a method used to bond people to groups, so observe the group's practices before you make a commitment.

There are a few reasons that so many newcomers, or even experienced Wiccans, go along with this. One is that some people are desperately looking for family. Many Wiccans are alienated from their biological families, and they may want to substitute the coven or group for the perfect family they're always seeking. Unfortunately, these people will usually go from coven to coven, leaving a group as soon as the members show themselves to be human beings with human frailties and emotions, and unable to live up to an impossible standard of perfection.

A more widespread reason is that some people want to attach themselves to a Big Name Pagan by taking the famous name. If the high priestess or priest goes along with this or encourages it, it isn't a good sign. Our Word for the Day in this case is *hubris*.

Initiation is dangled like a carrot as a reward for good behavior, or the high priestess or priest indicates that s/he will "take back" your initiation or clerical credentials if you do or say anything that displeases him or her. Initiation is not a bargaining chip, and it isn't a reward. Initiation is a shared promise between you and the gods, or—if you're being initiated into a coven—between you and the rest of the coven, with the gods as witnesses. I'm sorry to say that I've actually heard a priestess tell a candidate for initiation that he wasn't ready because he couldn't follow orders. The orders he was supposed to follow didn't have anything to do with Witchcraft; they had to do with obeying the personal whims of the priestess.

Another priestess was told that a covener was writing a book. She asked what it was about, and he told her. She said, "I'm not so sure I like that. I might have to take back your initiation."

At one meeting of a Wiccan volunteer group made up of people from different covens and Trads, a Third Degree Gardnerian priestess announced that she was going to be teaching a Wicca 101 introductory class. The priestess presiding over the group (not a Gardnerian, I might add) jumped right on her with the ferocity of a particularly nasty pit bull, demanding that the woman first submit her lesson plan to her, and telling her that there were certain things that she wouldn't allow the woman to teach. She then listed several things that any newcomer probably already knew, stuff that could be found in any beginner's book. It wasn't like it was a big Trad secret or anything; the HPs was simply exercising her control. She then threatened, "If I find out you're teaching any of these things, I'll pull your ministerial credentials." The prospective teacher was completely cowed.

Well, it was fairly appalling. I mean, since the prospective teacher was a high mucky-muck Third Degree and all.

Things like this are why I have my ministerial credentials through the good ol' Universal Life Church.

Initiation cannot be "taken back." During an initiation, the priestess simply performs the ritual that formally connects you with the gods. Once that vow is taken, it's between you and the gods, and only you can rescind it. If you are initiated into a coven, you might conceivably be banished from it or otherwise formally separated from it, but nothing can separate you from the gods except your own will. You can renounce the gods, if you eventually feel you must, but no priest or priestess or earthly power can do it for you.

There are a lot of banishings from the coven, or people are sometimes obviously favored over others, or made the butt of

jokes. If a coven is a family, this is a sure sign of a dysfunctional one.

No authentic priestess or priest, or coven for that matter, banishes any initiated coven member lightly. In the first place, it indicates a failure on the part of the priest or priestess. If someone has conned his way into your coven or has created enough trouble to be dropped from the group, then you, as priestess or priest, have made an error in judgment somewhere. Banishing involves someone who has been initiated: If he hasn't been initiated, he can just be asked to leave. But if someone reaches the point of initiation and the priestess or priest hasn't spotted the person for a phony by that time, something's wrong. If you, as a priest or priestess, feel that you can't initiate someone after she has completed the work or training, then you need to have a serious talk with her and come to an understanding, usually releasing her to seek elsewhere. Or sometimes an initiated coven member gets disillusioned and causes trouble. It happens.

One or two banishings can happen. When a coven has more than that, something is not only wrong, it's *seriously* wrong. And it goes back to the priestess or priest. Either she's incredibly naive about people, or she's running a very odd group.

There's a coven here in Salem that picks up and drops so many favorites that we call them the Baskin-Robbins coven: you know, the Flavor of the Week? Some favored candidate will be next in line to take over the coven and the whole spiritual shebang, she'll strut her stuff for a while, basking in the reflected glory and working her butt off for the high priestess, and then—bang!—we're all asking, "Whatever became of . . ."

Another coven had one member who also worked his butt off for the high priestess, but with a different result. This poor guy was the Rodney Dangerfield of Wicca: He got *no* respect. He would do anything to get his initiation, which was being put off endlessly. At one point, he was asked to dress up in a ridiculous costume at Halloween for a publicity stunt. Everyone, including the HPs, snickered, with the "Elders" saying, "I can't believe he actually did it!" and going off into hysterical laughter, even months later when they recalled the incident.

Real caring folks.

You must refer to the high priest or priestess as "my Lord" or "my Lady." Somebody's been reading way too many fantasy novels and hanging out at too many Renaissance Faires.

They try to dazzle you with highfalutin titles. There's a great old saying: If you can't floor 'em with the facts, baffle 'em with bullshit. And the more titles they have, the more watchful you should be of New Age cowpats.

Just about the easiest thing to achieve in Wicca is an exalted-sounding title: Nobody ever checks on them. For one thing, you can make up your own title. For another, if someone's got titles and initiations from numerous Trads, how come the exalted one couldn't stick with any of them? You might simply be dealing with a Poodle Witch,* but you're most likely dealing with an egomaniac.

One of my favorites in this category was a brochure distributed by people who claimed to have been "initiated and elevated to Third Degree in Coven A, initiated and elevated to Third Degree in Coven B, founding member of the Council of Nobles, Presiding member of the Council of Elders," and on and on.

There actually is a coven in Salem with a Council of Nobles, and every time I hear the phrase, I have to muffle a giggle. It just sounds so pretentious, like something from Monty Python. They also refer to their high priestess as "Dame" Somebody-or-other, leading many of us to break into singing, "There Is Nothing Like a Daaaaaaaame!" whenever we see her.

What people are saying with these long strings of grandiose credentials is actually, *Please, please take me seriously!*

---

*A Poodle Witch is one who just can't shut up about his or her exalted lineage, and claims to have the "papers to prove it." Just like a registered dog. May also be known as a "Charmin Witch": His or her "papers" are probably printed on single roll for First Degree, double roll for Second Degree, triple roll for Third Degree. This is in proportion to the amount of bullshit generated, hence the real need for all the paper.

Your work in Wicca, your treatment of those around you, and the opinions of your fellow coveners should be the only "credentials" that matter. People will take you seriously and grant you respect when you've earned it. And at that point, you don't have to ask for it.

Sex for Secrets

This is going to be short and sweet. An authentic Wiccan coven or teacher will never ask you to have sex with or for him or her, and will never ask you to do anything that makes you sexually uncomfortable. If any such request is made, you walk. Don't even think about it; get out and don't look back. And if there was non-consenting sex involved, *you've been raped.* Call the cops. Don't fall for that old "but it will make Wicca look bad" bullshit— nothing makes us look as bad as unprincipled people preying on others. Rapists need to go. Not to be indelicate, but I'll bet the Catholic bishops are wishing now that they'd been more vigilant about sex offenders.

Money for Nothing?

Here's a can of worms for sure. For years there's been a controversy over people accepting money for teaching Wicca. On one hand, you'll get those who say that you should never charge for anything connected with Wicca, and that includes teaching and divinatory readings. Some say no payment for teaching, but you should get paid for doing readings if you're doing them for people outside your coven. And there are those who hold that you should be paid for your time and experience, no matter whether you're teaching, reading, or what.

There's been an argument for paid clergy in Wicca, and some of the arguments are persuasive, but what hasn't been thought through very well is *who* is going to pay them.

Clergy in Big Religion have their salaries paid by the contributions of the congregation, theoretically through the collection plate. In reality, if they had to rely entirely on that, there'd be big trouble. That's barely enough for the building fund for the new church hall. That's why they hold fund-raisers and court those church members with deep pockets who can make big-bucks tax-deductible contributions. (That isn't to say that this doesn't happen in Wicca—it's just that our members don't seem to have that kind of money. Or guilt.)

Catholic clergy, in theory, own nothing. Those boys have taken a vow of poverty: Everything they have actually belongs to the church. If you see a priest driving a big black Merc, it usually belongs to the parish.

This vow-of-poverty deal is sweet, and available to us Wiccans, if we want to do it. You can legally incorporate as a church and give everything you own to the coven/church. All the money you collect goes to the coven/church, and it's all tax deductible. Any small coven that does this is foolish—considering how complicated it is, how fraught with IRS peril (which is one of the worst kinds of peril), and how volatile some covens are. But, you know, I thought I'd bring it up.

Most Wiccan groups just aren't big enough or prosperous enough to pay their HP or HPs a living wage, so the "paid clergy" argument remains just a theory. For now.

Among the priestesses, priests, and other Wiccan teachers who accept money for teaching, the second question is: How much do you charge? Again, there's a controversy. I can only give you examples. I taught for nothing for years, asking only for donations to offset the cost of renting a place to teach and printing the hand-out material. At one point, when I was out of a job and couldn't carry the costs myself, I asked ten dollars a week for a five-week course of training. That also helped cover the students who really couldn't afford to pay anything.

I know many, many Wiccan clergy who refuse to take *any* money for teaching. I know some who use a barter arrangement.

And I know some who charge three hundred to nine hundred dollars.

Worse: There are some who charge big bucks and then blow off half the classes, with no refunds, promising that they'll make them up later. Okay, anyone can get sick or an emergency can come up. But if this happens more than once, or your four-week class stretches out into four months, start screaming for your money back. People who tell you that a class is going to be every Friday for four weeks should make every effort to stick to the schedule. People have lives outside Wicca.

No matter what you're paying or not paying, you should ask up front what you're getting. Ask for a course outline. Ask if this instruction is in magic or Wicca (some teachers separate the two). Ask how many people will be in each class and how much personal attention you can expect. If you're studying with a coven, ask if this training will lead to an initiation; if it's a degreed Trad, ask if this will result in a First Degree. Ask what materials will be covered, and what, if anything, you're required to buy. (*Hint:* If you're taking a course in magic or Wicca from a store, I'd be a little wary about being required to buy a lot of stuff.) Ask what books you'll be required to read, and look them over before you commit to the class (if you don't agree with the books, you're probably wasting your time and the teacher's). Ask how long this training course lasts. If it goes on for years and it's not in a coven that requires the year and a day for each degree, you could be getting taken. Above all—*ask who'll be doing the teaching.* If you're paying a Big Name Pagan for an expensive course and you never see him or her because some flunky is teaching the classes, you may be able to get your money back, in court if nowhere else. If you're asked to sign a contract, have a lawyer look at it. This is rare, but better safe than sorry, especially if you're paying big bucks.

Realize that paying a whole potload of money doesn't necessarily mean that you're getting superior training. It may only mean that the teacher has a high opinion of himself or herself.

Secrets and Lies

More than once I've heard beginners (and even experienced Wiccans, though not as often) say that they wanted to study with such-and-such a teacher, but the teacher had asked the students to submit to things that seemed questionable at best and dangerous at worst. Rather than using common sense, the beginner was saying that it sounded like a come-on, but maybe s/he should just go ahead and do whatever the self-styled Great One wanted, because "if it turns out that he really does know Real Secrets, then I'll just kick myself!"

Are you people grownups or *what?* And by grownups, I mean anybody over the age of eighteen with an ounce of sense or an IQ in at least the double digits.

First, there are no Real Secrets that make you more of a Wiccan than anyone else. Your relationship with the gods is strictly between you and the gods.

Second, no teacher who is worth squat is going to require you to do anything that makes you feel ashamed or afraid or puts you in danger. And nothing should come out of the blue at the end of the course of training: If you're training with a coven, the teacher should have been preparing you for initiation, and should have taught you exactly what would be required of you by that particular Trad. If there was anything you really couldn't agree with, you should have had the chance to question it early on. Either some modification could be made, or, if it's something honestly required by the Trad, you would have the choice to leave. You *always* have the choice to leave.

Beware of anyone who says that you have to swear an oath and that if you break it or leave the group, terrible curses will descend on you. Beware of anyone who says you'll be shunned by the entire Pagan community.* You should tremble before their awesome power, you betcha.

---

*Anyone who's been Pagan for long will bust a gut at that one.

This whole thing about secrets is dicey these days, anyway. We're not in immediate danger of being jailed and executed for our beliefs or for practicing magic. Also, most "secrets" have already been published, especially of the Gardnerian and Alexandrian Trads, and they still seem to be doing all right, although they've complained about it enough. But is there really a need for secrecy when it comes to the Trad or group's beliefs and rituals? Everybody knows what the Catholics, Methodists, Mormons, and Christian Scientists are doing, and it hasn't made those religions less effective to their believers.

What most groups say they're afraid of is that if any initiates of the Trad become disgruntled, they can threaten to publish the coven rituals and oathbound material. That's happened more than once to many a group. What it is, is blackmail. Give me that advanced degree or make me a high priestess or change things my way or I'll leave and put all your Mysteries on the Internet. It's not only been threatened, it's been done. And when it *has* been done, the world didn't collapse. The group or Trad didn't either. The worst that happens is that some malcontent publishes your secrets and puts his or her name on them, touting them as his or her own invention. Then the legitimate Trad has a lot of cleanup work to do, telling the whole world that so-and-so's version is not the real thing. But if your Trad rituals and beliefs have already been made public, the plagiarizer just looks dumb. A big plus is that new seekers can evaluate your Trad *before* they join, to see if it's right for them, eliminating a lot of problems later.

In the past few years, I've come to believe that every Trad's basic rituals and beliefs should be out there and public. It would let people know about the beauty and diversity of our religion and show that we have nothing to hide.

The good part about not having secrets is to be able to say to the spiritual blackmailer, "So . . . go ahead. Don't let the door hit you on the butt on your way out."

The only secret that should be required is that you do not reveal the names of people in your group to outsiders. In theory, that's why we take Wiccan or magical names in the first place: We're supposedly honoring a tradition that no one in the group could give names to the Inquisition because they didn't *know* their actual names. Although, as we've seen, that may be a bogus factoid.

And the reason that the identities of your friends and coven-mates should be kept secret *now* is that, although execution for witchcraft doesn't exist in the United States anymore, discrimination most certainly does.

However, I don't know of any coven in which people don't know everyone's real names and half their most intimate secrets, including that little indiscretion in 1992 with a quart of peppermint schnapps and a pair of beach boys.

I sometimes work with a small group, the Alliance of Earth Religions, in which everyone is required to be out of the closet, mainly because we do the kind of community work that demands it. We have some secrets, sorta, but since we talk about them a lot, and we've done public rituals, you could hardly call them the Mysteries of the Ages. Obviously, we aren't the kind of group that could be easily blackmailed.

Not so a coven that contained a lot of public school teachers and child-care workers. You don't think these folks weren't absolutely paranoid about whom they admitted into the group? And for good reason, given the public attitude that "Wiccans are out to subvert our children!"

The Nature of Mysteries

As I touched on in a previous chapter, nobody can teach you the real Mysteries. Mysteries are revealed to you, and only to you, by the gods. The nature of the Mystery is personal and revelatory. You could tell this Mystery to others, but it would be absolutely useless to them. All training is really a preparation to communicate with the gods.

This is the core of spirituality. It is a personal epiphany that cannot be duplicated, taught, read in a book, taught by mail or in a class, or experienced by a group. That's why we say, "In silence is the seed of wisdom gained."

You can join a coven, you can collect degrees, you can buy a dozen robes and amethyst wands and crystal balls and tarot cards, you can cast spells, you can have a library of occult lore out the wazoo, you can claim direct descent from the ancient ArchDruids. But until you hear the voice of the gods, you know nothing of real value.

How do you discover the Mysteries?

I have no idea. I know what happened to me, but it won't be the same for you. All I can tell you is that if you love the gods, and you spend some time in silence and ask for help or guidance, you'll get an answer.

And anyone who says that they can teach you this, or speed the process, or "channel" the information for you is lying to you and probably to him- or herself.

11

Three Things That Definitely Mark You as a Beginner

If you're a beginner and you're looking for credibility in Wiccan or Pagan Circles, never say the following: "My grandma was a Witch," "I have an ancient Book of Shadows," or "I'm a shaman." Trust me on this: Unless you're a stand-up comic looking for laughs, you're bound to be disappointed.

Every Witch who's been around for some time has a funny, disparaging story to tell about a newcomer who uses one of these three old tales. Most Witches won't say it to the seeker's face (although if they did, tactfully, it would save him or her some possible embarrassment later), but these lines are right up there with "I'll respect you in the morning" and "the check's in the mail" as all-time groaners. Even if they're *true*, nobody believes it. Most of the time, these lines are greeted with a momentary silence as the experienced Wiccan struggles to choke back several unsuitable responses. Or just tries not to hurl.

So why do people insist on saying these things? Several reasons. First, they want to quickly establish credentials as real Wiccans. Why they do this is beyond me: Whether you're Wiccan or not is between you and your deity. If you say you're Wiccan and you're not hurting anybody or anything, you got my vote.

Second, they want to impress you with their so-called power. These folks just don't get the entire concept.

Third, they feel insecure or unsure about joining a new group and don't want to be thought of as inexperienced—even though they are. I don't know why this is something to be ashamed of. *Everyone* was inexperienced at one time: I don't care if you learned Wicca at the feet of Gerald Gardner himself, you were still a beginner once. So, hey . . . go right ahead and *admit* you're new at this! Most Wiccans like to help beginners. It's fun to teach someone something new and hone your own skills and knowledge in the process. You learn by teaching, we sometimes say.

But people who approach Wiccans with the I-know-it-all attitude are dismissed as people who are not serious. There's an old saying: "Those who know don't tell and those who tell don't know." Unless they're volunteering to teach, that is. Or, you know . . . writing a book.

"Grandma was a Witch."

This is number one on the bullshit index. If there were as many witch grannies as claimed, the woods would have been full of old ladies dancing around every full moon and the churches would have been empty. Because this claim has become so pervasive and so laughable, many people are modifying it to "my granny had these . . . well . . . *powers*. Of course, the family never talked about it because they had to pretend to be good Catholics." Or Baptists, or Methodists, or whatever.

It may have been a big secret *then,* but you just can't shut them up about it *now.* They can't wait to out poor old Granny. According to these folks, Granny passed on her vast occult knowledge but swore little Taliesin or Morgana to silence. Grandma sure put her faith in the wrong hands, I tell ya, because these folks make sure you know all about her and her sorcery the first time you meet them. They never tell you exactly what Grandma taught them, but it was hundreds of years old and passed on through many, many generations, usually from the member of the family who was "burned at the stake." (They all have a crispy-critter ancestor.) Some people have actually claimed to be descended from people who died during the Salem trials, thinking that this gives them A+ magical references. Now, this is something that really frosts my cookies, because the accused in Salem were Christians and not witches. For Witch wannabes to use these unfortunate people in order to establish their own dubious credentials is pretty low-rent. The real giveaway is when they say that their Salem ancestors were burned. I mean, the least they could do is read some history before they try to con you.

These folks want you to know that they're only interested in your coven or your class or study group because they're "comparing techniques." Otherwise, they imply, they wouldn't waste their time with you unenlightened louts.

Yeah, right. Then, at their first Circle, they're totally bewildered by the simplest things. Apparently Granny, with all her Witchy knowledge, never taught them so much as how to cast a Circle.

Now, all of that said . . .

There is indeed a new generation of young people whose parents or grandparents came into Wicca during its earliest growth period in the 1960s, especially in America. These people are usually initiated into their parents' own Tradition. If not, they have enough religious knowledge to know that "Granny was a witch" is one of the more dubious stories connected with Wicca.

The Ancient Book of Shadows

This is another one that gets a big laugh at Wiccan gatherings. Perhaps the most accurate description of Wiccan reaction to the "I have an ancient Book of Shadows" theme is found in Rosemary Edgehill's excellent mystery novel, *The Book of Moons*.

The main sticking point here is that the term *Book of Shadows* first came into use with Gerald Gardner no earlier than about the 1930s—and that's pushing it on the early side. Although Gardner claimed to have adapted his rituals from earlier texts, he was never able to produce them, and he admitted that he'd filled in the gaps himself.

Another thing is that Wicca has always maintained that it stems from ancient agricultural festivals practiced by heathen people—people who could neither read nor write. So an ancient book of written rituals is pretty much of a stretch.

If there were any ancient Wiccan books, believe me, Wiccans wouldn't be hustling as much as they do to find old roots to lend legitimacy to the religion. If such existed, it wouldn't stay a secret. In fact, it would probably have been published as soon as it was discovered—for such is modern Wicca.

The main appeal of Wicca is that there *are* no standardized written rituals that would lead to a dogma. Most Wiccans take great spiritual comfort in using rituals that they have either written themselves, or adapted from friends or from people they admire, or from whatever anthropological data they can find. Any sincere religious ritual is valid, whether it's five thousand years old or only written five minutes ago, if it means something to you and brings you closer to your gods.

And you don't need any ancient book to do that.

"I'm a Shaman!"

When a beginner says this, it's just ridiculous. To be a real shaman takes years of study, self-discipline, humility, and work, plus a fairly rigorous physical discipline. The original qualification to be a shaman was to have had a kind of psychotic break, a complete disassociation with reality that let you cross over into another consciousness. And this was not done with drugs: It was a naturally occurring phenomenon, thought to be the touch of the spirits. You might or might not come back from it, mentally, but you were a direct conduit with the divine.

Plus, most of these instant shamans claim to be Native American—in this country, anyway, because they're the only indigenous shamanic culture around. Of course, ripping off Native Americans is a time-honored custom among us white folks, but until the New Age began, at least we'd left their religion alone. (That's not to say that there aren't shamanic groups that draw their rituals and philosophy from other cultures, but they're not claiming to be Native American.)

For a time, inspired by the books of Lynn Andrews and others, middle-class white people just could not wait to spend a weekend at the Res, absorbing the culture and coming back to the suburbs to rave about their spiritual rejuvenation and their animal totems. And make no mistake—their animal totems are always eagles, owls, wolves, or bears. You never hear of anybody's having a totem woodchuck.

If they're women, they talk about how they are now Medicine or Warrior Women. If they're men, they talk about the physical rigors and how only Real Men can stand the initiation rites. (It is curious that these new "shamans" are unable to show you their scars.) They all claim that they have varying degrees of Native American blood, usually from whatever tribe seems trendy. Right now, it seems to be the Lakota, since the Mohegans are busy gleefully paying back the white man by taking all his money at their casinos.

When some New Agers found that they could chug drugs and claim it was a religious rite, suddenly everyone was a shaman and connecting to the Great Spirit, whom they apparently took to be a stoner, too. This was considered totally cool: You could get really, really wasted and claim it was all in the name of religion. The local Lutheran Bake Sale just couldn't match *this* experience. Well . . . depending on what they put in the cookies.

You can easily spot these Suburban Shamans at New Age gatherings: They're the smelly ones with the glazed eyes and the endless and unintelligible drug rap. They sound like Charlie Manson on crack.

While it's true that many shamanic traditions used peyote or other hallucinogens to enter altered states of consciousness, this was done in a strictly religious setting within a specific culture. It isn't something that you can accomplish on a back-to-nature weekend with the other trendoids.

And don't think the real Native Americans aren't pissed off about this whole thing, either. Many legitimate tribes have condemned, or at least discounted, some of the books purporting to be written by shamans, and have taken understandable offense at their religious culture being watered down and packaged to the Soccer Moms, hotshot marketing executives, and druggies.

If you want the true shamanic experience in the framework of Wicca (and it's out there, but it isn't for the faint of heart), find out more about the Faery Tradition, the Trad begun by Victor and Cora Anderson. (See chapter 6, on Traditions.)

The latest development in this trend is the adaptation of Voudoun as the plaything of the spiritually seeking middle class. Voudoun is one of the most ancient of the world's religions and is still practiced in many places, mostly unchanged from its original African form. It is a religion that was carried by African people to the strange places in the world where they found themselves sold into slavery. Kidnapped from their homelands and families, brutalized, starved, and dumped on the very dubious mercy of strangers who did not even speak their language, Africans managed to hold on to their sanity by holding on to their religion, even if the only place they could practice it was in their hearts and minds. Even when forced into Christianity and told that their former religion was officially evil on a stick, the Africans held their beliefs. That took courage.

Now many African-Americans are rediscovering Voudoun, peeling away the layers of misunderstanding that Hollywood and racial bigotry have piled upon it. Many are traveling to Africa and Haiti to learn more and are discarding the Christian symbolism that believers were forced to adopt in slave times. Voudoun is fast regaining the respectability that was stolen away from it by racism, fear, and lies.

So naturally, the trendoids are beginning to claim that they're Voudoun practitioners, learning the names of a few of the *loa* or *orishas,* and drawing a couple of *veves,* maybe buying a snake.

But as with most things, the fakes will get bored and move on, and the true believers will persevere and advance the religion.

The moral of this story is: If you're a beginner, step right up and say so! You'll be surprised at how many people will be willing to show off their own wisdom by sharing their experience with you and helping you along. As an extra, added bonus, no one will give you a hard time about messing up in ritual or forgetting what Element is associated with what direction. You can make mistakes and everyone will be jumping up and down to be the first to tell you what *they* would have done and what's the real, true way to do whatever it was you were doing wrong. We Witches live for this stuff! You're doing us a favor, so don't be shy about saying you're new. You'll get lots of attention, and an indulgent chuckle when you mess up.

Try getting away with that when you've claimed that Grandma was a Witch who received her ancient Book of Shadows from an old shaman. Who practiced Voudoun on the side.

12

Fifteen Things Everybody Knows But You

(AND ONE THING *NOBODY* SEEMS TO KNOW)

If you're a seeker, new to Wicca, you might be a bit confused by the lingo. Actually, some of us who have been around are sometimes confused, too, but you'll never hear us admit it. This should probably have been titled "Fifteen Things Everybody Thinks S/he Knows" because some of our most entrenched ideas are based on faulty folklore. In this chapter you'll find a random collection of Wiccan wisdom and observations, some of which you might not know, some you may already know, and some explanations that just might surprise you, no matter how long you've been practicing. And be sure to check out the part about the Wiccan Rede: Unless you're a biblical scholar or a philosophy student, this information about its possible source might be news to you. It sure as heck surprised me when I came across it.

"The Craft"—Why We Call It That and Why We Shouldn't

The Craft sounds to me like basket weaving or making cute little things out of twigs and dried flowers. It's a real catchall term: Both

Witches and Wiccans refer to it to describe whatever it is they're practicing, but it's most often Wiccans who refer to Wicca as the Craft. This seems to be working against our own purposes: Wicca is not a "craft," it is a *religion*. If we want it to be respected as such, perhaps we should think seriously about losing this term.

So where did this "Craft" idea originate? The explanation I hear most often is that it refers to "Witchcraft," but like so much of Wicca, it was lifted from Freemasonry. When you refer to the Craft, you should more properly be referring to the practices of the Masons. Wicca and Freemasonry are superficially very much alike, because Gerald Gardner was a Mason. No surprises there.

There is some historical reference for the term, though. In Old English, *wiccecraeft* is derived from the words *wicca* (masculine) and *wicce* (feminine), meaning "someone who practiced sorcery." And, by the way, *wicca* is pronounced witch-a, not wik-ka, but this mispronunciation is something we're stuck with by now.

I've heard Wiccans tell people that *Wicca* means "wise man" or "wise woman," but that isn't true. The closest match to "wise man or woman" would be the word *wizard,* which is derived from the Middle English *wis,* which *does* mean "wise." Jeffrey Russell, in *A History of Witchcraft,* says that the word *wizard* first appeared about 1440, meaning "wise man" or "wise woman," and that in the sixteenth century it referred to a practitioner of high magic; only after 1825 did it begin to equate with *witch.*

Many Wiccans will tell you that the Craft refers to "the craft of the wise" because the root of *wise* is the same as the root of *Wicca.* As we've seen, it just ain't so. I've also heard Wiccans say that *Wicca* is a Celtic word meaning "the craft of the wise." Not accurate either. Actually, almost none of the words relating to craft, witch, or Wicca is Celtic.

Magic, Magi, and Magicians

If you're referring to someone as a *Magus,* then you're really saying that he's a Zoroastrian, a practitioner of the ancient Persian religion that has survived into the present day. (The Parsis in India are Zoroastrians.) The word comes from the Greek *magos*, which referred specifically to a hereditary Zoroastrian priest. *Magic* and *magician* derive from French *magique*, Latin *magia*, and Greek *mageia*.

Magick, Majick, Majik

Actually affectations, as in "Ye Bok of Ye Arte Magickal." Every time I see this spelling, I think of prim ladies running Ye Olde Antique Shoppes. It's just *so* precious. I've also heard it referred to as "TolkienSpeak." Why do so many Wiccans sound like they live in a fantasy novel?

The usual excuse is that the *k* is added to distinguish what Witches and Wiccans do from stage magic. Oddly enough, stage magicians don't use the term *magic* much themselves, and usually describe themselves as *illusionists,* since what they do certainly isn't magic; it requires great skill and years of practice.

The spelling is supposed to have originated with Aleister Crowley, the P. T. Barnum of the occult set. Whatever Crowley was practicing, it sure wasn't Wicca, and if he were here, he'd be the first to say so. While the spelling might be part of the historical heritage for ceremonial magicians who follow Crowley's principles, especially Thelemites, it really doesn't belong in Wicca. And nothing looks wackier than someone referred to in print as a "magickian." Usually, people use the spelling because they think it sounds more occult or shows the world that they're in the know, privy to the real secrets, Big Time Serious Witches.

You're not necessarily more magical just because you can't spell.

Newbies

This is a word used to describe those who are new to Wicca. Unfortunately it's most often used rather insultingly, usually by those who have forgotten that they were once clueless newcomers themselves. I prefer the words *newcomer* or *seeker* (not in the Harry Potter sense) because these people really are seeking something. Whether they find it in Wicca remains to be seen, but we should give them the courtesy of taking them seriously. People who condescendingly use the term *newbie* with a sneer remind me of high school cliques.

Pointy Hats

It's really hard to pin down the reason that Witches are associated with pointy hats. One explanation is that the conical hat (without a brim) was a mark of a heretic: Apparently, the church gave you a free hat—just before they killed you in order to save your soul. Not all heretics were witches, but for sure all witches were heretics, so there you are. Goya painted some famous pictures of accused Spanish heretics wearing their conical hats and tunics, both bearing occult symbols.

Another explanation is that the Puritans, famous in the Massachusetts Bay Colony for their singular attitude toward witches, wore peaked hats. Actually, these were pointy hats without the point: They went up a ways, then the last part of the point was lopped off flat. This hat was simply the fashion of the times: Everyone wore them, even the people who were hanged as witches. Even King James I, who made witch killing a national sport, and Matthew Hopkins, who turned witch finding into a very profitable, if despicable, career. These hats became firmly associated with witches because the drawings and engravings made during this period showed everyone, witches and witch persecutors alike, wearing them.

In Salem, we have a statue of the town's founder, Roger Conant. Old Roger's wearing the ultimate in Puritan fashion for 1630: a high, semipeaked hat and a sweeping cloak billowing out behind him. Tourists crowd around him, standing in the middle of the street, snapping pictures and holding up the four-way traffic on

North Washington Square, because they're convinced that Roger is a Witch. Of course, it doesn't help Roger's image that he's standing right in front of the Witch Museum. It gives us Witches a big giggle at Roger's expense.

There's a wonderful photo on some recent popular greeting cards of a bunch of little old ladies having tea in an outdoor garden. They're all in dark clothes wearing conical hats with wide brims. Naturally, most people assume they're Witches. They're not; they're little old Welsh ladies wearing traditional folk costumes. They *may* be Witches, but probably not. You'd have to check to see if they're wearing pentacles, too.

Broomsticks and Flying Ointment

Okay, enough with the claim that Pagans rode around the fields on broomsticks, jumping up as a charm to let the corn know how high it should grow—and that's how the broomstick came to be associated with witches.

The broom has long been a symbol of domesticity. Roman midwives used to sweep the doorsteps of houses where a child had just been delivered, to drive away evil spirits. In Romania and Tuscany, brooms were stashed under the bed to *repel* witches.

The earliest printed picture of a flying witch appeared in Ulrich Molitor's *De Lamiis* in 1489, and showed the witch flying on a cloven stick. In fact, the stick was thought to be the most common medium of transvection (flying), the second most popular being the staff. The broomstick didn't really make its lasting mark as a flying machine until about 1580, when Jean Boden (*Démonomanie*) associated it with witches. Early woodcuts also show witches riding wolves, goats, oxen, and dogs, all of which were supposedly preferred to the stick. They probably would have been more comfortable.

During the Middle Ages, the ancient Teutonic Valkyries, the majestic warrior women who rode through the battlefields and chose the heroes for Valhalla, became degraded to witches, and their great battle steeds to broomsticks.

British scholar Rossell Hope Robbins said that the broomstick probably won out as a flying tool because of its tradition as the symbol of women, like the pitchfork is a symbol of men (we should start including that in the Great Rite: "As the pitchfork is to the male, so is the broom to the female"), and because of its phallic symbolism. How something can be a female symbol and a phallic symbol at the same time is one of life's little mysteries, but I guess it kind of synthesizes the idea of female/male polarity.

There were tales of witches who left the house at night to go frolic with the Devil, that satanic stud muffin,* while fooling their husbands by leaving a broomstick on their side of the bed. Those must have been *some* anorexic babes.

One thing the witch hunters all agreed on was the flying ointment. This interesting stuff first cropped up in Apuleius's *The Golden Ass,* in which a woman anointed herself and transformed into an owl. Later, it cropped up in almost every accusation and trial of witches after about 1460.

It's funny that, when women flew, with or without a broom, it was considered witchcraft and resulted in death. When men did the same thing, it was considered a miracle and resulted in canonization. Saint Joseph of Cupertino was supposed to have made seventy flights, in front of witnesses, one of them the Spanish ambassador.

If people wanted to prove the phenomenon of flying witches, all they had to do was look at the record. An early writer on the subject, named Limborch, said that you only had to look at the number of witches who confessed to flying to the Sabbats, "which would never have been done, or suffered by the popes, unless these things really did happen." Yeah, and I saw Santa over my house, too, but nobody's burning *him* at the stake.

---

*See chapter 2 for the salacious details.

Pentagrams, Pentacles

The pentagram has become the corporate logo of the Wiccan religion, sort of like the Cross for Christianity and the Star of David for Judaism. Pentagrams are slapped on mugs, T-shirts, key chains, and just about anything else that can be manufactured for mass consumption.

How did the pentagram, the five-sided center of a five-pointed star, and the pentacle, a star in a Circle, become associated with Wicca? Simple. Like much of Wicca, they were imported from ceremonial magic and alchemy. The pentagram is pretty old: Its use as a powerful symbol was firmly established by Pythagoras, and jewelry bearing pentagrams has been found dating from the Roman Republic. In fact, author Raven Grimassi has a fabulous Roman pentagram ring, and if I ever meet this guy and see him wearing it, I plan to arm-wrestle him for it.

Deosil, Widdershins

Deosil is to move clockwise in the direction of the sun's movement; *widdershins* is to move counter to it. According to accepted Wiccan wisdom, you cast a Circle by moving deosil and release it by moving widdershins. And like most things in Wicca, other people will tell you that you never move widdershins while doing magic, no matter what, lest you offend the gods or practice black magic or some such terrible calamity.

Cowans

Same thing as muggles. If you don't know what a muggle is, you just haven't been paying attention to pop culture. *Cowan* is a Masonic word denoting those who are uninitiated into the Craft of the Masons. This entered the Wiccan vocabulary with—three guesses!—Gerald Gardner.

The Cone of Power

This is actually a simple visualization for sending out magical energy. The idea is that everyone in the Circle forms the perimeter of the bottom of a Circle, projecting energy into the center, which narrows and concentrates as it rises into a cone that goes out into the universe to do the magical work when the cone is released.

The Charge of the Goddess

What is now known as the Charge was thought to have originated in Charles Godfrey Leland's *Aradia or the Gospel of the Witches,* first published in 1890. In this passage, Aradia, the daughter of the Queen of the Witches, sent to earth to teach the secrets of sorcery, makes her promise to her followers:

> When I shall have departed from this world,
> Whenever ye have need of anything,
> Once in the month, and when the moon is full,
> Ye shall assemble in some desert place,
> Or in a forest all together join
> To adore the potent spirit of your queen,
> My mother, great Diana. She who fain
> Would learn all sorcery yet has not won
> Its deepest secrets, them my mother will
> Teach her, in truth all things as yet unknown.
> And ye shall all be freed from slavery,
> And so shall ye be free in everything;
> And as the sign that ye are truly free,
> Ye shall be naked in your rites, both men
> And women also . . .

This evolved into the more familiar prose version of the Charge of the Goddess when it was revised and greatly expanded for Gerald Gardner by Doreen Valiente. The Charge is now the centerpiece of many Wiccan rituals, and priestesses of long standing can usually rattle the entire thing off from memory, so well and flowingly is it written. For the full version of the Charge and the ritual into which it belongs, read Stewart and Janet Farrar's *A Witches Bible Compleat.*

An earlier inspiration for the Charge, and possibly for *Aradia,* is found in Lucius Apuleius's *The Transformation of Lucius Apuleius of Madaura, or The Golden Ass.* This excerpt is from Robert Graves's 1951 translation:

> I am Nature, the Universal Mother, mistress of all the elements, primordial child of time, sovereign of all things spiritual, queen of the dead, queen also of the immortals, the single manifestation of all goddesses that are. My nod governs the shining heights of Heaven, the wholesome seabreezes, the lamentable silences of the world below. Though I am worshipped in many aspects, known by countless names, and propitiated with all manner of different rites, yet the whole round earth venerates me . . . The primeval Phrygians call me Pessinuntica, Mother of the gods; the Athenians . . . call me Cecropian Artemis . . . for the trilingual Sicilians, Stygian Proserpine; and for the Eleusinians their ancient Mother of the Corn. Some know me as Juno, some as Bellona of the Battles; others as Hecate . . . the Egyptians . . . call me by my true name . . . Queen Isis . . . Only remember and keep these words of mine locked tight in your heart . . . that you are dedicated to my service. Under my protection you will be happy and famous, and when at the destined end of your life you descend to the land of ghosts, there too in the subterrene hemisphere you shall have frequent occasion to adore me.

It is very interesting to read the entire Charge, especially the second half, and then to read the Apuleius version. It is from the Charge, and obviously from the earlier Apuleius, that Wicca has adopted the idea of a single Goddess under many names. (See chapter 3, on deities.)

The Great Rite

A subject of many a Wiccan in-joke, but actually a very solemn ritual celebrating the male and female energies that are present in all living things. Literally speaking, the Great Rite is sexual intercourse between the earthly representatives of the Goddess and God (usually the high priestess and high priest), symbolizing the union of male and female. The Rite is used to raise great magical power. The Great Rite is most often performed in a symbolic sense, with the high priest plunging an athame (ritual knife) into a chalice of water or wine held by the high priestess.

Negative Energy

This is one of the most misused terms in Wicca, and really infuriating when it's used by the smug and self-righteous, which it is all the time. You'll hear the Wiccan equivalents of Dana Carvey's famous Church Lady sniffing, "Oh, she just gives off such negative energy!" when what they really mean is "I don't like her." But it isn't Paganly Correct to say such a thing (nonjudgmental religion, remember?), and besides, talking about energy makes you sound more psychic.

Negative is not a synonym for *bad* or *evil*. Negative energy is just like positive energy, opposite sides of the same thing: You need both halves to make up the whole.

The Summerlands

Contrary to much Wiccan lore, the Summerlands is not an "ancient Celtic" idea of heaven. The Summerlands is part of the religion of Spiritualism. According to Barbara Thurman, president of the National Spiritualist Association of Churches, "*Summerland* is a term used by Andrew Jackson Davis to describe the Spirit World/ Heaven. Davis was a forerunner of Modern Spiritualism and founded the Children's Progressive Lyceum. The Spirit World is not necessarily a place of rest. It is a real world, just like this physical world with everyone occupied with something, but I assume that since Davis named it Summerland, it was always bright, and sunny as a pleasant summer day might be."

It's interesting about the Summerlands: It sounds identical to the Plain of Asphodel, one of the three parts of the Roman underworld, where the shades of the dead continued to go on about their business.

Fluffybunnies, Fluff, White Lighters

All derogative terms, and frankly, undeserving of the prevailing scorn. Fluffybunnies are those Wiccans and/or Witches, almost always beginners, who see Wicca and magic as all sweetness and light, ignoring anything that they consider "dark" or "negative." Most Wiccans who use this term have been fluffybunnies themselves at one time. (See *newbies*.) Having said that, fluffybunnies can actually do some harm to themselves or others in attempting to "send white light" to people and situations about which they know little or nothing. A good rule is: "Never attempt to do magic, even if you consider it good magic, unless you know the whole situation."

You see the term *fluffybunny* applied to Scott Cunningham's books. This pisses me off, because there's no reason to knock Cunningham's work. It's an excellent way for seekers to start, because his books don't favor one or the other Trad, and emphasize safe, ethical magic. They're kind of like primary school books in that you have to learn to walk before you can run. As a seeker reads farther into Wicca, he or she will come to learn the more complicated aspects of the religion soon enough. Many a snooty Wiccan *now* conveniently forgets that he started with Cunningham *then*.

And now . . . something almost nobody knows *except* you.

The Wiccan Rede

There are almost as many versions of this as there are Trads that use it, but the most familiar form is, "An ye harm none, do as ye will." Ask ten Wiccans where it came from and maybe seven of them will tell you that Gerald Gardner adapted it from Aleister Crowley's "Do as you wilt shall be the whole of the law; love is the law, love under Will." Maybe he did and maybe he didn't, but a similar phrase appears in a much earlier version: "Love, and do what you will," from Saint Augustine.* Yeah, I was surprised, too. Some later church fathers, just to be on the safe side, I guess, added a word to Augustine's original text, changing it to "Love *God,* and do what you will," but in the original, it's: *Dilige, et quod vis fac.* The word *dilige* is Latin for "esteem" or "love." The phrase has also been translated as *Ama, et fac quod vic,* using the Latin *ama* for love—but that word means a different kind of love.

Considering how much Augustine hated Pagans, there's a kind of neat poetic justice in all this.

That about wraps it up, friends and neighbors. If you're ticked off by now, I've done *my* job. But I'm hoping that some of the opinions expressed in this book might strike a chord with you, especially if you consider Wicca as a religion, a framework for spiritual enrichment, and if you take joy and comfort from the everyday observances, large and small.

We have a wonderful opportunity to establish our religion as one to be respected, so that no Wiccan ever has to be ashamed or afraid to admit to following it. If you can be vocal about your religion, that's fine, and your efforts may benefit us all. Just don't forget that working quietly in the background is just as effective.

*Tract 7, *On the Gospel of Saint John.*

The most important thing you can do for our religion, and for yourself, is to remember the gods, to honor them and strengthen your connection with them, sharing power between you. It's not one of those shepherd-sheep deals, it's a divine partnership maintained by love and respect, not guilt or fear.

How many other religions can say that?

The Usual Appendix

I'm only listing the resources I used as background for this book; the groups that I've worked with and know personally (or someone I respect vouched for them); and the Web sites I've found useful or amusing. If this were a complete list of Pagan resources, you'd need a forklift to get this book off the shelf.

Bibliography

Ancient Wisdom and Secret Sects, Mysteries of the Unknown series, New York: Time-Life Books, 1989.

Baigent, Michael, Richard Leigh, and Henry Lincoln. *Holy Blood, Holy Grail.* New York: Delacorte Press, 1982.

Birks, Walter, and R. A. Gilbert. *The Treasure of Montsegur: A Study of the Cathar Heresy and the Nature of the Cathar Secret.* London: Crucible Books, 1987.

Cavendish, Richard. *The Black Arts.* New York: Perigee Books, 1967.

Drew, A. J. *Wicca for Men.* Secaucus, N.J.: Citadel Press, 1988.

Gardner, Gerald. *Witchcraft Today.* London: Rider & Co., 1954.

Herzberg, Max. *Myths and Their Meaning.* London: Allyn & Bacon, 1928.

Hutton, Ronald. *The Triumph of the Moon: A History of Modern Pagan Witchcraft.* New York: Oxford University Press, 1999.

Julianus, Cassius. *50 Things You Can Do to Advance Pagan Religion.* Wells, ME.: The Julian Society, 1994.

MacMullen, Ramsay. *Paganism in the Roman Empire.* New Haven: Yale University Press, 1981.

Robbins, Rossell Hope. *The Encyclopedia of Witchcraft and Demonology.* New York: Bonanza Books, 1981.

Robinson, John J. *Born in Blood: The Lost Secrets of Freemasonry.* New York: M. Evans & Co., 1989.

Russell, Jeffrey B. *A History of Witchcraft, Sorcerers, Heretics and Pagans.* London: Thames & Hudson, 1980.

Seyffert, Oskar. *The Dictionary of Classical Mythology, Religion, Literature, and Art.* New York: Gramercy Books, 1995.

Spence, Lewis. *The Encyclopedia of the Occult.* London: Bracken Books, 1988.

Taylor, John M. *The Witchcraft Delusion in Colonial Connecticut.* Heritage Books, 1989.

Wilson, Colin. *The Occult, a History.* New York: Random House, 1971.

Web Sites and Organizations Mentioned in This Book Or Just Listed Because I Like Them

Covenant of the Goddess, www.cog.org

Circle Sanctuary, www.circlesanctuary.org

Lady Liberty League, www.circlesanctuary.org

Nova Roma, P.O. Box 1897, Wells, ME 04090, www.novaroma.org

The Julian Society, P.O. Box 1897, Wells, ME 04090,
www.juliansociety.org
A group dedicated to advancing Pagan religion.

The Sisterhood of Thalia, two places at once and not anywhere at all, MA
This group defies description.

McFarland Dianics, www.geocities.com/mcfdianic

Church and School of Wicca, www.wicca.org

Our Lady of Enchantments,
http://members.aol.com/lady51366/oloe.html

Universal Life Church, www.ulconline.com

The Temple of Brigantia, www.janeraeburn.com/brigantia
A Wiccan coven in Maine honoring Celtic-Roman deities and offering rituals and apprenticeships to the Maine Pagan community.

Betwixt and Between Community Center, Dallas, Texas,
www.betwixt.org

Aquarian Tabernacle Church, www.aquatabch.org

American Civil Liberties Union (ACLU), www.aclu.org

People for the American Way, www.pfaw.org
    Join up. Keep the Religious Right from sneaking up on us all.

Covenant of Unitarian Universalist Pagans (CUUPS), www.cuups.org

Witches Against Religious Discrimination (W.A.R.D.),
    www.ward-hq.org

Witches League for Public Awareness (W.L.P.A.), www.celticcrow.com

Connecticut Wiccan and Pagan Network, www.cwpn.org

Iseum of Hidden Mysteries, www.sacoriver.ner/~anubis
    The Iseum honors the ancient Gods of Egypt, practicing Egyptian
    magic through the use of ancient texts and prayers within a context
    relevant to modern life. It offers classes, networking, education, and
    public outreach programs. The Iseum is a member of the Fellowship
    of Isis, a worldwide nonprofit organization that honors the Goddess
    and God in all their forms.

Clan of the Dragon, www.geocities.com/jkarrah
    An online book of draconic rituals and magic, blended into a tradi-
    tional Wiccan framework.

Dragons of the Fire Mountain Clan, www.kerowynsilverdrake.com
    Like dragons? You'll want to see the beautiful dragon pics and links
    on Kerowyn's excellent site.

BeliefNet, www.beliefnet.com

The Witches' Voice, www.witchvox.com

Cherry Hill Seminary, http://cherryhillseminary.org

Neopagan.com, www.neopagan.com
    A useful site by A. J. Drew, author of *Wicca for Men*.

Circle of Souls Radio, http://circleofsouls.net/radio/
    Pagan news and great music!

Salem Tarot, www.salemtarot.com
    A useful site with info on the Salem witch trials, a visitor's guide to
    Salem, also a nifty online three-card tarot reading (it's addictive).

Serious Resources

The Texas Pagan News has details on the Dallas City Council invocation
by Bryan Lankford. For pictures and the complete text of the invocation,
go to www.txpn.org/Content/dallas/invocation

The Principia Discordia
Yep, they put it online. No words can do it justice; you'll just have to read it: http://www.ology.org/principia/body.html

"The Scholars and the Goddess" by Charlotte Allen, *Atlantic Monthly,* January 2001. May be read online at
    http://www.theatlantic.com/issues/2001/01/allen.htm
This article infuriated Wiccans when it appeared, and for good reason. Allen is a Christian scholar, whom many thought was simply out to discredit Wicca. She says otherwise: that she only meant to challenge the antiquity of the religion. Those Wiccans who are serious about religion will want to read it, however, and will also want to read the rebuttals from Wiccans that appeared in the April issue at
    http://www.theatlantic.com/issues/2001/04/letters.htm

Roses and Thorns: Pagan Poetry by Angel
The poem "The Halloween Witch" paraphrased in chapter 7 is by this poet. I haven't been able to locate the author, and I hesitate to reprint a copyrighted work without the author's permission. I received a copy of it in e-mail from the Reverend HP Heru Gawen at Circle of Souls Radio, who saw it on an Internet newsgroup. If you're out there, Angel, we really like your work. *Get a Web site!*

Humorous Resources

Lady Pixie Moondrip's Guide to Craft Names
One of the most hilarious guides you'll ever read, and everything you need to decide on your very own "Craft" name.
    http://www.turoks.net/cabana/CraftNames.asp

The Random Craft Name Generator
If you don't want to do the arduous work required to use Lady Pixie Moondrip's guide, the folks at the Flinders University Pagan Association have devised a Random Craft Name Generator to do the work for you!
    http://www.turoks.net/cabana/CraftNames.asp

You may be a Redneck Pagan
Have you ever hollered, "Skeeter! Get on over here and cast this here Circle!"? These folks have some other funny stuff on their site.
    http://www.accessnewage.com/articles/humor/redneck.htm

How many Gardnerians does it take to screw in a light bulb?
    http://www.accessnewage.com/articles/humor/redneck.htm

Why Wiccans Suck

Holy cats. Somebody needs some Prozac and a nice nap. And I thought *I* was bitchy.

http://www.angelfire.com/fl2/4nongoths/backup/index.html

Index